W9-AYE-940

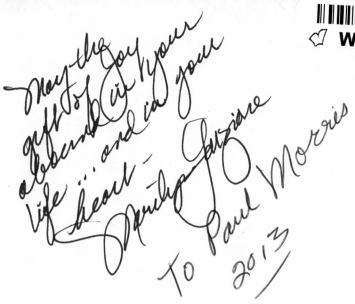
May the
gift of joy
abound in your
life ... and in your
heart —
Marilyn Gustave

To Paul Morris
2013

WHAT PEOPLE ARE SAYING ABOUT
RELEASED TO THE ANGELS

Released to the Angels helps readers understand the experience of
Alzheimer's not only through the eyes of a caregiver but also through
the eyes of an individual with the disease. Marilynn takes you along as
she and Patrick find strength, humor, beauty, joy, and finally peace in
the everyday moments that comprise their story. Caregivers will find
the book to be full of keen observation, wisdom, and laughter ... I will
not soon forget this remarkable love story or its inspiring message.

Elaine Sproat, President & CEO
Alzheimer's Association
Hudson Valley/Rockland/Westchester, NY Chapter

"Marilynn Garzione has written a beautiful and loving tribute to her
husband, Patrick. It reveals deep compassion and understanding and
should be read by anyone dealing with this terrible disease."

Senator William J. Larkin, Jr.
New York, 39th Senate District

"...as inspiring as a double rainbow."

Sovella Tankersley

"Those of us who are living with this illness can understand it better
as we read of others' managing well with prayer and patience and,
of course, love. Upon finishing the book I was left with a quiet
understanding of an honest and real love and "caring" ... it was so
calming and so real."

Frann Jazombek, caregiver

Released to the Angels

Discovering the Hidden Gifts of Alzheimer's

Marilynn Garzione

iUniverse, Inc.
New York Bloomington

Released to the Angels
Discovering the Hidden Gifts of Alzheimer's

iUniverse Star
an iUniverse, Inc. imprint

iUniverse books may be ordered through booksellers or by contacting:

iUniverse
1663 Liberty Drive
Bloomington, IN 47403
www.iuniverse.com
1-800-Authors (1-800-288-4677)

Because of the dynamic nature of the Internet, any Web addresses or links contained in this book may have changed since publication and may no longer be valid. The views expressed in this work are solely those of the author and do not necessarily reflect the views of the publisher, and the publisher hereby disclaims any responsibility for them.

ISBN: 978-1-936236-20-6 (sc)
ISBN: 978-1-936236-21-3 (ebook)

Library of Congress Control Number: 2010932921

Printed in the United States of America

iUniverse rev. date: 8/6/2010

*To Patrick, whose heart touched mine
and never let go.*

Contents

Acknowledgments

The writing of this book is not only the result of the journey Pat and I shared together, but also includes the many wonderful people who played a role in helping to bring our story to others. To those who were there for us, who gave us support, and to those who then took part in this book's publication, I will always be grateful.

Thank you:

To Dr. Lisa Valow and Dr. David Jaeger who, both in talent and in support, gave your all in helping Patrick. In so doing, you gave me precious time to share with him. I will always be grateful.

To Janet, Ann, Dennis, Darlene, and all those at Orange & Sullivan Hospice who were there to help me during hospice care. To Theresa and Doreen, who came through snowy, icy storms to show me how to give injections and offered a shoulder when I failed miserably in my attempts. Those visits meant more than you could possibly know.

To Elaine, Michele, Gina, Meg, Wendy, Ruth, Pam, Shelly, Dinah, Camille, Andy—and all those associated with the Alzheimer's Association who accepted me with open arms into the family of those who know and understand. Thank you for opening the door to a greater understanding of this disease and for your unending efforts to ensure that someday we will find a cure. It will happen … it must happen.

To Mica, who, with incredible talent, can create beauty through a lens and joy in life around her.

To Sherri, who, with incredible sensitivity and love, cared for Patrick in my absence. Little did you know that in those times you became my caregiver, too.

To Joan, who, through your love and acceptance of your brother, also accepted me. You and Pete have been a source of strength and support. Thank you.

To Suzanne Houston, who wrote such beautiful words of encouragement at a time when I truly needed them, and who then worked with me to quote the beautiful words of others. Thanks!

To Rich, for building a firm foundation of support.

To Denise. You, too, have felt the pain of loss. I gained from your dignity, your grace, your loving heart. *Merci mille fois, ma chère amie.*

To the 'young uns'—Christine, Stephanie, Matt, Suzanne. Your laughter, your energy, your hugs are gifts I still love to open. Thank you!

To Phyllis, Jeannie, Sandy, Becky, and 'Catalina.' Those discussions, advice, and laughter were as delicious as our luncheons! Thanks!

To Kay … a neighbor, a friend. I am honored that you are both. Thank you for letting me borrow a cup of love and support any time I needed it.

To Ida and John. Forever thank you for your wisdom, love, and daily prayers.

A Maite: Estabas conmigo cuando éramos jóvenes, cuando yo no sabía la profundidad del amor que iba a crecer en mi vida. En los años después, cuando había mucha distancia entre nosotras, eras tú quien no sabías el soporte ni el amor que nuestra amistad me dió. Gracias mi amiga.

To Julie. The Weston Priory … a simple gift of music, a wonderful gift of friendship. Thank you.

To Jeannie and Diane, who, through the years have helped reveal a deeper, more meaningful definition of being sisters.

To Mom, who, by example, showed me what love is willing to take on so that life can be celebrated. You cared for Dad, and your strength served as a guide that helped me as I cared for Pat. Mom, we will carry their love forever in our hearts.

To Bryan, Nick, and Sue, for the laughter, for discussions over a dining room table and the unconditional acceptance of friends. I am so grateful for our friendship and for the love we all shared with Pat. And not to be forgotten … thank you, Mr. Peabody!

To Cami. Years have given us time to truly test the meaning of joy, pain, and love. Our friendship has grown with us so that now we can look back and know the strength it provides. You were there, Cami, for me … and for Pat. I take comfort in that and, more, in the joy of our friendship.

To Susie. You knew Patrick in those early years; you came to love him—to laugh, smile, and share with us. For what he taught us, we are better. And when you add that to the love we have shared between us, it is no wonder that we call ourselves friends. Forever.

Introduction

Alzheimer's is devastating. It can erase memory, change lives, and destroy dreams. As with other life-threatening illnesses such as stroke or cancer, Alzheimer's affects not only the victim but the caregiver as well.

Trust me. I've been there. Any caregiver will tell you that as time goes by, the sense of self often becomes lost in the needs of another. I found myself in a maze of responsibilities that robbed me of strength and any hope that life would ever be normal again. For one thing, I had to find a way to face the sometimes unthinkable challenges that faced me every day. The cleaning up of adult incontinence accidents can leave you frustrated and discouraged. Emotional outbursts, inappropriate adult behavior, and anger are but a few of the behaviors that face you every day. And often, after the endless routine of bathing, feeding, administering medications, and comforting, you realize that you have no energy left to care for yourself. Couple all this with up-in-the-night confusion and attempts to escape the house, and you have a clear glimpse into the daily routine of someone trying to care for a loved one with Alzheimer's. It is no wonder that anyone faced with this is left exhausted and desperate for relief.

Yes, Alzheimer's has power to affect your life. But I have found that, while the disease is beyond our control, there is in fact, a choice. We do not have control over the power of Alzheimer's, but I believe we do have a choice as to how we *react* to this disease. We are given all sorts of moments to react to—moments of pain, moments of despair, moments of humor, moments of joy. And if we react to the positive moments and assign to them as much power as those moments of pain, then we have taken a step toward not being defeated by a disease or condition that imposes itself upon us or our loved ones. Sometimes those moments are so subtle that they may go unnoticed, overlooked. But they are there, too. And if we open ourselves to them, I truly believe that we can begin to see that in and around this disease, life is still going on. With that awareness, we can then honor that life and treasure the joys that are given us.

In reading this story, you will share in the daily routines, emotions, and feelings that are a part of caring for a loved one with Alzheimer's. You will also experience what many caregivers have referred to as "jumping" in time—the almost involuntary experience of being in the present and being instantly transported to the past by a triggered emotion or memory. Many entries reflect this jumping phenomenon, which may very well be a coping mechanism that brings temporary relief from stress by offering sanctuary in the past.

I write this book as a way of sharing with you my affirmation that life offers both pain and joy—and the opportunity to feel both. It is my hope that as you read our story you come to realize, as I have, that laughter is just as much a part of Alzheimer's as are tears, frustration, and all the human emotions we experience in the face of tragedy and sickness.

My message to those of you who are caregivers is that you will be surrounded by pain, yes, but you will also be surrounded by moments that contain quiet gifts of humor, joy, calm, and acceptance. Hang onto them. Hang onto them with strength and the trust that they will sustain you as you go through this journey with your loved one.

Marilynn Garzione
Caregiver

Part I

Looking Back from Now

God granted us memory so that we might have roses in December.

—J. M. Barrie, *Courage*, 1922

Morning

I've always loved snowy mornings. It seems the whole world has created a softness so fragile a single footstep would shatter it completely. For a while, at least, the illusion is complete. But even as you look out, you know that this beauty is not going to last. As much as you want this moment to stay forever, the world will take on the reality of passing cars and, with it, the untouched whiteness will disappear. This morning as I look out the window I smile, knowing that soon my day will begin. I will put my cup of coffee down, walk into the bedroom, and, as I have done for so many mornings, I will introduce myself to my husband.

Patrick has Alzheimer's. Where once I couldn't bring myself to even pronounce that word out loud, I am surprised that over the years it has lost its power, and I, in turn, have lost my fear. I don't know when it started, but the horribleness of this death sentence has given way to memories that have their own strength. Could it be that I have simply chosen to ignore its harshness, to make my own definition, my own reality?

It doesn't matter. Whatever answer I come up with, I will, in the end, open my eyes to see that my day is still here and that there are things to be done.

It wasn't always like that.

He Was

I don't always like to think back. A strange thing to say, but when you live in a present that contains past losses, you tend to create a cushion that lessens the pain of comparison. Yet so much of the present that is good begins in the past, and so I let myself remember.

Patrick was, and is, a man who has journeyed through life with all the self-doubts, joys, and memories that accompany any journey. He was a child who grew up in the New York community of Newburgh. He was a boy who found time to read, encouraged by a mother who took pride in education and an Italian father who willingly labored to provide for his family. He was a brother who grew up with his four sisters and gained from their experiences, keenly aware of the fact that he was the only son and oldest in the family. He was a youth who lingered in the library to look through magazines with pictures of soldiers and chaplains killed in World War II. He was a young man who was affected greatly by the sacrifices of others and who chose to follow a commitment.

He was a Catholic priest.

The Road Taken

I remember clearly the first time I met Patrick. My family was stationed at Ramey Air Force Base in Puerto Rico in the mid-1960s, where my father was the Protestant chaplain on base. Patrick was the Catholic chaplain working side by side with my father. As a teenager in high school, I was bewildered, yet fascinated, by this priest who did not fit the mold of what I thought a religious would be like. He didn't speak in pious tones, he was incredibly funny, and he seemed quite fond of rum and Coca-Cola. Yet he would spend hours at our kitchen table with my father, laughing, discussing the Bible into the wee hours of the morning. The fact that their religions were so different didn't present barriers. In fact, it probably was because of those differences that my father, a Lutheran minister and a chaplain in the military, chose to get to know this New York Italian. Both were sincere in their beliefs; both were accepting of each other's. But above all else, both genuinely liked each other. Theirs was a deep friendship that was to last until my father's death in 2000.

And I was growing up, admiring this man who had become so close to my family, yet curious. He, in turn, acknowledged my existence, my youth, my immaturity. Yet even when I would sometimes join in on those kitchen table discussions, he would never ridicule my youthful utterances, choosing instead to listen and then guide me to logic and understanding. As the months and years went by, he became a friend—someone I knew I could count on in the years ahead. His journey had long begun. Mine was just beginning.

Somewhere along the way, our paths would meet again. Little did I know how long our journey together would be.

The Chef

Yesterday I wasn't feeling well. A cold was coming on, and every muscle ached, giving me full indications that the next few days would not be pleasant. It wasn't enough to stop me, but enough to be irritatingly noticeable. This morning I woke up unable to talk, but ready to start in despite a miserable sore throat and an overall feeling of malaise. Pat immediately noticed my condition and instinctively tried to care for me (a throwback to the years when he cooked all the meals, handled everything, and, in general, spoiled me rotten.) He demanded that I stay in bed and insisted that he was going to cook breakfast. The thought of this was not exactly comforting, since I can't really trust him with the stove. But then he announced that he was going to prepare "that round thing with white on it." A list of culinary possibilities flashed through my mind, and then I smiled ... a bagel with cream cheese! Since it would require no cooking, I figured we were in safe waters, and I nodded approval. So I lay back and let him take over. I have to admit there was a moment of doubt there when I was trying to explain the difference between the refrigerator and the freezer (the bagels were in the freezer) and also what marmalade was, but I was confident he could handle this. After he left, I heard the clatter of dishes and pans and knew that whatever appeared would be from his heart.

I was not disappointed. After what seemed like an eternity, he appeared with a tray and a nice bagel with cream cheese and marmalade piled on top. He was so proud. I felt this great feeling of love and comfort knowing that, in spite of the losses, he still was trying to take care of me.

It was the best frozen-solid bagel I've ever eaten.

Love

On Wednesday I took Pat to the card section of the supermarket to pick out a birthday card for me. Despite the fact that Alzheimer's robs you of the daily things you take for granted, there still exists the need to follow rituals: gift giving, the expression of feelings. I have found that by doing these things, a kind of normalcy remains, and with it comes a kind of stability.

Long ago Patrick lost his ability to decode letters and writing. I led him to the stack of cards, knowing that if he saw a card he liked he could at least express himself in that way. So there we stood, in front of the section where all the cards for wives and sweethearts were. I showed him the limits and parameters of the cards he could choose from as I ran his hand along the edge that indicated the demarcation between birthday cards for sons, daughters, mothers, etc. I told him to pick out a card that would be something that he thought I would like for my birthday. I had shopping to do, so I told him to take his time, that I would be back in a few minutes. I could see that he took an immediate interest and barely paid attention as I left him.

When I returned I knew he had accomplished his mission. He proudly held up the card that he had chosen with a dignity that expressed his sense of accomplishment. Today, my birthday, I opened my card. It was mine, something he had picked out for me, something that had caught his eye among all the others. I'll never know what caused him to choose this particular card—perhaps a color, perhaps his feelings for me. But I was touched. On the front was an image that conjured up feelings of love and romance ... a big rose with a heart, undoubtedly the very thing that caught his attention. And then I read the words etched in silver against a black background. They read:

"To the Special Man in My Life"

... not quite the sentiment I would have chosen, but good enough.

Impact

How do you measure twenty years? Do you measure the days, the passage of time? Or do you measure what those years have done to you as a person, or what you have done for others? I cannot measure the twenty years that Patrick was a priest. But I do have glimpses of what he was then, what he did, and what others saw in him. I do know that he helped a young couple adopt a baby when all paperwork had failed. I do know that while stationed in Taiwan he used his spare time to organize the local people and gather material to build an orphanage. I know how he worked with the homeless and drug addicts of New York City's Bowery. I know of countless times he gave comfort and counsel to others.

What I don't know, what I never asked about, was the extent of his inner doubts, the self-questioning that went into his decision to leave the priesthood after twenty years.

In the early years, I reacted only to feelings expressed. I remember a particular letter he wrote to me during his military stay in Vietnam. It was during the Tet offensive, a particularly difficult time of heavy fighting. As a chaplain, he traveled from camp to camp, unarmed, traveling with the soldiers as they fought in the jungles and rivers of the Mekong Delta.

His letter described a horrible day. Many soldiers had died in only a few hours, and, as a priest, Patrick was there to administer Last Rites. He wrote of holding a dying soldier in his arms, of grasping his hand and hearing his screams of pain. The soldier died calling out for his mother, and Pat felt the impact of not being able to help or comfort him. After a morning of death, in a desperate attempt to clear his mind, he set out on a walk around the inner perimeters of the camp. As he walked he heard a soft noise, like a low whimpering. On the ground to the side of the road he saw some corrugated tin roofing, and he knelt and lifted the metal. He saw a touching scene: a mother dog had just given birth to puppies. In one instant he felt the painful irony that here, in the midst of all this death, was new life … and, releasing all the frustration and weight of the day, he cried.

It was not until several years later that Patrick would leave the priesthood. By then, I am sure I was a part of that decision.

Realization

Even as a teenager I was never a teenager. I always preferred the company of adults, and I loved conversations that searched for meaning and purpose in life. I very much loved to laugh, but was never the frivolous type and viewed the typical teenage quest for independence as silly. Even in college, the weekend binge parties were not my thing. I found pleasure in the company of others who, like myself, were more intent on self-definition than on self-indulgence.

With Patrick I could express myself freely. Our correspondence began as I entered college, and in some respects it became a continuation of the long conversations once held at our kitchen table. In good times and bad, we shared humorous anecdotes, his observations of daily life, and my joys and tribulations of growing into adulthood. When I was sad, he was there. When something gave me great happiness, those feelings were shared. A mutual respect grew. What I, and he, either didn't realize or ignored was how close we were growing through our correspondence. As years passed, we began to examine our feelings. Our letters became a way of sharing, a way of caring.

It was apparent to me that of all the men I had met and was continuing to meet, he was becoming, at least subconsciously, the only one I wished to share with. Emotionally I didn't know what to do with those feelings. I think, to some extent, I buried them, preferring to not address the full extent of my feelings.

My emotions were safe, hidden away.

Safe Ground

Time always leaves its mark and often reveals what lay hidden in the past. With time, I grew to understand that it was not only I who found comfort in our closeness. I began to see how Patrick, too, looked to me for responses and reactions to thoughts and beliefs. He trusted my input and relied on my acceptance of his feelings. By nature he was always there for others, but I knew he took comfort in the fact that someone was there for him. A safe ground grew between us.

For a long time humor easily diffused any serious feelings we felt for each other, and the distance inherent in our letters established a natural line we did not cross. Yet it was a struggle to not express what had grown between us.

I remember once, on a rare visit, we were looking at some snapshots. I was standing behind him as he sat at the table. I reached down to pick up a photo while my other hand rested on his shoulder. It remained there just a few seconds too long. I was embarrassed and withdrew my hand. But in that instant I was keenly aware that he knew my true feelings for him.

And, deep down, I knew his. It was hard to face what had now come to the surface. Though for a long while we tried to ignore how we felt, there came a time when we finally expressed openly what had been held in so long. There was a joy in knowing that we loved each other, but an awful feeling that this was something we couldn't have. For months we did not correspond, genuinely trying to suppress what we knew and felt. But, inevitably, in moments of weakness or need, one of us would call or write, and the intensity of our feelings continued.

Feelings that, slowly, quietly, were becoming a permanent part of our lives.

The Decision

Despite the love we held for each other, or perhaps because of it, Pat and I agreed that we had to separate. It was difficult to accept that his life was not meant to go in this direction. I made a decision that if I loved him, I had to love him enough to live without him for the rest of my life. I realized finally that I had to start again, and to do that, I chose to create distance between us. At the time I was finishing work on my Master's degree in foreign language, and the idea of living in Spain took root; it would give me that distance and a new beginning. I arrived in New York City en route to Madrid. It felt good to be in the same state, the same city where Patrick lived. But there was one place I had to go.

It was morning when I walked through the doors of St. Patrick's Cathedral. I sat in a pew toward the back, far enough away from the sound of tourists walking past and close enough to the front to feel a part of this place where Pat had been ordained so many years before. And I made a vow that I would stay there until I was sure, absolutely, that I could give him up. Through the morning and afternoon, I struggled between prayer and tears … a strange mixture of pleading, anger, and love. And finally I left, exhausted, knowing that I had given back what I couldn't have.

Some things are too painful and personal to write here. Let it be said that I lived in Spain, learned a great deal, loved the culture, and planned for my future. I'm not sure if in my heart I had truly lived up to my vow to give him up, but some things are decided for you. Unknown to me, Patrick, too, had come to a decision, and it was then that I received a letter stating that he was coming to Spain to see me.

What should have been a romantic reunion wasn't. It was a painful, soul-searching session that went into the wee hours of the morning. But from that agony came the realization that, whether right or wrong, from human frailty or strength, for whatever the reason, we would be sharing our life together.

I once had asked Pat if, as a priest, he was ever lonely. He said, "No," and then, pausing, said, "… Well, the only time I ever feel alone is after Midnight Mass on Christmas Eve, when everyone leaves to go home to their families. I have no family to go home to." And at that moment I knew that if God were to ever allow that we marry, we would choose Christmas Eve, so that he always had a family to go home to.

Vows

Our decision to marry came after years of friendship, years of searching, questions, doubt, and, finally, certainty. The train ride out to Idaho was for me both exciting and romantic. I was going to be a bride! I was going to marry the one person I had always loved, someone eighteen years older, my mentor, my best friend, my companion. It didn't matter that we had no money for plane tickets. The train was a slow, romantic journey that I was sure would end with us living happily ever after.

Patrick, who was always playful, was looking out the window of the train in solemn thought. Looking back through a filter of years and gained wisdom, I realize how, despite our decision, this had to be hard for him, a giving up, a decision that meant no looking back. Where my world was surrounded with a romantic glow, his world was suffused with a far more serious tone. He turned to me and, seeing my thoughts, immediately smiled.

Dad and Mom met us at the station to drive us out to their cabin in the mountains surrounding the town of Sandpoint, Idaho. Dad practically ignored me as he hugged Pat and immediately began talking about the books he was reading, the philosophy of this, the dichotomy of that ... whatever. Mom, in her wise way, guided me to the car, knowing that Dad was too excited to think of anything but the chance to catch up with his old friend. The next few days were filled with excitement as Mom and I busied ourselves: making our wedding cake (she's a fantastic cook), walking into the woods with Pat and Dad to cut down a tree for Christmas, and talking quietly in the evening.

And then on Christmas Eve, with the snow falling outside, my father married us. Included in the ceremony was a green ceramic chalice that had belonged to Patrick and which we had brought with us. It was a simple ceremony, with a personalized homily that Dad had written for us and vows we gave to one another.

It was not until we arrived home that I discovered the chalice. It had been broken on the return journey. Without a word being said, Pat repaired it and placed it in our home, where it is today. I know there are those who will, no doubt, assign great symbolism to this, but it is for me more a symbol of imperfection, of repair, of healing. It says to me that nothing can go back to what was, but if we choose to accept what is now, that too can be precious.

Beginnings

Our married life began. I was teaching Spanish at a local high school, enjoying the day-to-day involvement with the kids and learning valuable lessons and skills that would become important in later life. Pat, on the other hand, was working as grievance co-coordinator at the prison located on the grounds of what was formerly Pilgrim State Mental Hospital on Long Island. His skills as counselor and listener came in handy, and he easily related to the prisoners. His sense of humor and easygoing manner won him friends among his colleagues.

Our personal life was typical of many newlyweds. We had little money, so we found other ways to build our home. Although Pat was never very proficient at carpentry skills, he managed to build a stable, if somewhat lopsided, bookcase/entertainment center. I tried my hand at domesticity by sewing curtains and choosing coordinating colors for our living room. He pampered me, fixing meals and giving me the time to pursue my interests in painting and piano. Joining our household was a tiny canary that Patrick brought home one day and promptly named Ludwig Van Tweethoven. True to his noble name, he filled the apartment with his own brand of music. From the very beginning we continued our established routine of long talks, long walks. Every Saturday morning we would go out to McArthur Airport to have a cup of coffee, talk, and watch the planes take off and land.

Simple pleasures. Simple times. His playful humor was the perfect balance to my more serious attitude, and because of our age difference, I gained a lot from his positive outlook on life. He, in turn, probably smiled at my youth and inexperience.

We were happy ... and why wouldn't this go on forever?

The Italian

Years ago, we had been watching *The Godfather* when it was first shown on TV. At some point I turned to Pat and asked if he thought there was anything to the stereotype of Italians that seemed to be promoted in the movie. He laughed, "Well … yes and no. I don't know about the Mafia stuff. But one thing … family. There's a strong thing about family or people we love. We would do anything to protect them. You're my girl. I wouldn't let anything or anyone hurt you. If they did, they would have me to contend with."

Family. Love. Protection. My family is Norwegian. There was a strict, if not somewhat stoic, acceptance that we loved each other, but there was not an overabundance of expression. Patrick, however, could easily express his feelings toward me, and I, in turn, eagerly soaked up his love. I liked being protected. I liked being his. A hunger for affection: Throw in a glass of wine, some *pasta carbonara*, a couple *cannoli*, and you pretty much had the complete package.

The Dance

Today some music came on, and I couldn't help but invite Patrick to dance with me. I have always loved music, and to this day I can't help but play it on the piano or feel it in dance. In all those years Pat never wanted to join me on the dance floor, his reluctance stemming, no doubt, from the fact that dancing was not part of the curriculum in the seminary. But now, with all inhibitions lost and feeling the rhythm of the music, he joins me. There are no dance steps, just a gentle rocking back and forth, with him reacting to my guidance and steps.

Alzheimer's creates a kind of slow, gentle dance. Pat will follow my lead; if I am happy, I will see him trying to share in that, laughing and smiling as I do. If I am sad, he reacts to that, too. And the times when I'm agitated, he becomes confused, afraid. There are exceptions to this, but at this stage in the disease, it is becoming the norm. It comes to me that I am his link. I am his only connection to what is left of his reality. If I choose to destroy that, I could do so, easily. So I find that I calm myself in order to calm him. This does not come easily. It is a choice. It is a deliberate lesson I have chosen to learn, and I am not always the model learner. In the past it was he who offered a strength I could draw from. It was he who made decisions. I reacted. And so, where once he calmed me, now I am the one who speaks low and gives reassurance.

A slow dance that has come full circle ...

Flowers

For as long as I have known Patrick, he has loved flowers. I, on the other hand, have never had a green thumb. Early in the year, he would diligently plant the flowers out front, water them, and do whatever it takes to finally produce a panorama of color. I must say I have always appreciated his efforts, even though I have never tried in any way to cultivate the green creatures. So this spring I decided I must, in some way, try to keep up the garden, not only for Patrick. There was a keen impression of abandonment, made clear by the fact that our front flowerbed was overgrown with weeds. I didn't have the slightest idea of how to go about it, but figured the local nursery is equipped and prepared for non-believers such as I. So we trekked out to the greenhouse and together picked out a couple of trays of baby impatiens. Then, with a bucket of water, some Miracle Grow, a spade, and a kneepad, we set to work.

I asked Pat if he would like to do the honors of digging and planting, but, alas, he was confused. It was evident that this would be my first horticultural adventure. Pat stood behind me as I dug the little holes. He would then hand me a baby plant from the tray of flowers I had placed on the ground next to him.

I must say, I was rather pleased at my progress and was gaining confidence every minute. Pat, too, seemed in his element. There we were, moving down the line, planting as we went. I would dig, reach back so Pat could hand me a new plant to put in the hole, pour some Miracle Grow and water on it and, voila! move to the next spot. Only when I got to the end of the line did I permit myself the luxury of standing up to survey all that is good. I started to laugh.

The first tray of plants was empty. Pat had then reached to the earth and ever so gently removed the baby impatiens I had already planted … and, one by one, had handed them to me to replant.

The Photo

Yesterday I found an old picture of Pat when he was a boy. In the photo, he was dressed in a little sailor's outfit, standing in his yard, squinting against the sun. I asked Patrick who that was, seeing if he would recognize himself. "It's a child" was all he said.

I have often wondered what he was like as a child. Did he play marbles? Was he afraid of the dark? Did he play hooky? In years of health I asked him many questions, but now I have so many more. From what others say, I know that he was quiet and obedient; if someone put him on the sofa and told him to stay, he would. He loved running. He had a Mickey Mouse projector that he played until it broke. I have a mixture of memories, both those Patrick has told me and what older people in his family remember. Time, for him, is moving backward. And as it does, all the defenses that we form as adults disappear. This disease will never give you back what it has taken. But I am learning that if you can let go of the man, you can have the child. I never knew what he was like as a boy, so in a way this is a discovery.

And the glimpses of the child I see are endearing.

Exiled

I had been outside trimming the bushes. It was a gorgeous day, and over the sound of the electric trimmer I was busy humming. Patrick was inside watching television. In typical fashion, my mind was already on the next task, something I knew I would enjoy far more than this job that had always belonged to Pat.

A sharp pain brought me back to reality. At first it felt like a pin had somehow opened in my blouse, but that was impossible. Then a dozen pins, a thousand. In an instant it didn't matter. I knew. At first I tried to brush the yellow jackets off my arm, but to no avail. Incredibly, they just kept coming. I started running, and instinctively I headed into the house. Just get the things off! I had the presence of mind to know that I couldn't yell, that Pat would be upset, but I could hear sounds coming involuntarily from me. At that moment Patrick realized I was in trouble and started toward me. I only had a second to decide. I ran, yellow jackets and all, into the tiny corner bathroom next to the garage and slammed the door. And there I battled, not at all the victor. And Pat stood on the other side of the door, yelling to tell him what was happening. Strangely, I felt a strong anger that he was there when all my focus was on this assault on my body. Somehow this was my battle, and if he couldn't do anything to make it go away, I didn't want him there. I was able to escape the bathroom with only one yellow jacket managing to slip past the closing door. I had been stung fifteen times on my arm.

In the following days, despite a bad reaction to the shot they gave me in the emergency room, I healed. And Patrick was there, no longer shut out. Every day he would participate, demanding to look at my arm—the swelling, the redness. He felt better, I think, knowing that he could share my pain.

Cooking

Pat was an excellent cook. His father had been a caterer, and from what Patrick has told me, his mother had the ability to taste a dish and reproduce it in her own kitchen. Pat, having lived alone for so many years, easily managed a kitchen too and created recipes to die for. Fond memories abound of him cutting garlic, parsley, and herbs to put into a tomato sauce that would be bubbling on the stove as the pasta boiled in water mixed with a few drops of olive oil. Presented with semolina bread and a glass of wine, the meal was perfect! Any time I craved something, he would magically emerge from the kitchen with his offering, and I, the taster, would delight in his culinary endeavors. I handled the Thanksgiving and Christmas turkey, but the day-to-day cooking was out of my realm. I was helplessly inept and spoiled. To this day I have an irrational fear of cooking, due in part to the fact that those around me could cook so well.

Today I fixed a lentil soup. That has always been his favorite, and, with that in mind, I set out to prepare a delicacy that he would be proud of. When I tasted it, I must admit it tasted good, and I proudly set it in front of him at the table. Pat has always been my best critic. I don't know why his approval is still needed, but it is. And through the years, as I stumbled with recipes, it was Patrick who always encouraged me. Even when the results were less than optimal, he would always find something good to tell me so that, sensitive as I am, I could take heart from the fact that he found it edible. "Marilynn, why don't you try this …? Maybe next time you could throw in a little …" It was always enough to let me know I was on the right track but needed just a little refinement. I've noticed in these last months how his tastes have changed. Where once he chose herbs, whole grains, little sugar, now he hungers for anything sweet, creamy. It's ironic that he's come over to my side; I would kill for a cinnamon roll or *pasta alfredo*.

Pat tasted my soup. Stripped of language, his communications are now presented with raw honesty. After one spoonful, he looked up at me and said, "No … awful … crap."

Well, Emeril I'm not.

The Movie

I'm the type who loves to watch a favorite movie over and over, like listening to a favorite CD or watching reruns of *Seinfeld*. Pat, too, loves to watch movies; for him, forgetting does offer him the warped advantage of being able to see something fresh each time. So tonight I put on a movie we hadn't seen for years. It was the Sidney Poitier/Rod Steiger classic, *In the Heat of the Night*. Popcorn popped, sofa blanket ready, we were prepared. The movie began. Patrick was immediately engaged in the opening scene, and I could see that he would enjoy, at least in part, this old movie.

And then it happened. In the middle of a scene, Rod Steiger, with a heavy Southern accent, turned sarcastically to his co-star;

"Virgil. That's a funny name for a "boy" from Philadelphia. What do they call you up there?"

What followed was the powerful response of two voices speaking in unison:

"They call me Mr. Tibbs!"

Patrick shouted out the next line in a clear, unmistakable voice. I actually jumped as I listened to him, word by word, recite Poitier's part. Then came another scene, and sure enough, Pat responded verbatim, with the confidence of an actor delivering his appointed lines. I was fascinated, spellbound. In normal conversation, Pat can barely express himself, and yet here the words came easily, in an articulate flow of expression.

What is it about this disease that lets you remember some things so clearly, while others are gone forever?

Embarrassment

Patrick always loved to be silly. Sometimes he would go to goofy lengths to get me to laugh. Whenever we entered an empty elevator, I knew what was going to happen. As soon as the doors closed, he would start laughing, grab me in a feigned passionate kiss, and not let go. Then a split second before the doors opened, he would suddenly release me, stand up straight, and assume an air of dignified innocence. It happened every time. There were the times in the supermarket when we would be walking down an aisle, and he would start what I could only call his "Snoopy dance." Embarrassed, I would beg him to stop, but he always enjoyed making me laugh, especially in public.

Once we were in the car, slowly driving through a residential area. I happened to glance over at him. There he was, driving the car with a spiral of chewing gum hanging from the tip of his nose. He didn't say a word. He simply continued driving, waiting for me to respond. So I bit my lip, forcing myself not to laugh, and turned to look out the window. It didn't matter. He kept looking straight ahead, knowing I knew. Finally, I couldn't stand it any longer and burst out laughing, "You know, Pat, you wouldn't do this in public. If you didn't have me as your audience, you wouldn't do this!"

I should have known better. Without saying a word, he rolled down his window and waved to a man walking his dog. I reached over and begged him not to, but he began asking the man for directions. I was dying from embarrassment. The gentleman approached our car and gave a startled look when he saw this grown man with gum hanging from his nose. Pat gave no indication that anything was unusual. He simply faced and listened to the man who, now trying to control his laughter, started giving directions. After holding in my embarrassment as long as I could, I finally blurted out, "I'm sorry, sir. It was a dare" at which point the gentleman began to laugh. Pat then thanked the man and rolled up his window. Only when we were alone did he burst out laughing.

And now the silliness is gone. Recently we were in New York attending the revival of *42nd Street* on Broadway. Despite not being able to understand everything, Patrick was enjoying himself. And then, as an old favorite started playing on stage, he began to sing out loud. It lasted only a few seconds, but as I watched others looking and then staring at him, I simply smiled at the moment.

I was not embarrassed.

That Night

None of us go through life without pain, without loss. I have found that questioning why brings no comfort. But I *have* found that sometimes pain can bring out strengths, however hidden, until we reach a time when we can look back in wonder at how we never knew we had those strengths all along.

Many years ago on an April night, I was alone in our condominium on Long Island. Patrick was upstate, and I was readying myself for bedtime. An ordinary night, an ordinary sleep. But the hours that followed would change our lives forever.

I woke up, startled by movement and darkness. Above me on the bed was an intruder who held a knife to my throat and yelled at me to shut up, to not make a sound. It took several seconds to realize what was happening. By that time, I knew this was bad. I remember the pen flashlight, the smell ... the knife. It hurt. He pressed the long edge of the knife into my throat and said he was going to kill me. I then heard the ripping of duct tape and felt the tightness of it being wrapped around my head, closing out the only light I could see. I could hear him going to the phone, the slight jingle of bells as he slammed the phone back on the table (he had cut the wires). And then he came back to me.

Nothing flashed through my mind, no pictures of my childhood or review of my life. Instead came a sickening, horrible feeling that I would die with my eyes closed. It wasn't the violence of the rape. It was knowing that in twenty minutes I wouldn't be breathing. But strangely, there was no fear. Instead, there was numbness and disbelief that this was really happening, and a quiet voice that came to me to lie still, to not antagonize him. It was as if I shut out everything. There was no time, no feeling. I was suspended in a kind of protective blanket.

I will never know why he left me alive. I have fuzzy images of the hours that followed: of the police in the room, of Patrick bursting through the door, of him being restrained while the two officers tried to calm him, of Cami, my friend, trying desperately to shield me from the pain.

And my world collapsed.

Lost

I was lost. And Pat was lost, too. Here was a man whose whole life fostered the belief of giving and forgiving. And yet, as my husband, he would have killed to protect me. I know a part of him was destroyed, replaced with guilt at not having been there. But in those first few months, and even in the following years, I had nothing in me to give, nor could I help him escape those feelings. We both had to face anger and pain. And through it all, it was he who struggled to give me a hold on life, to somehow help me find a way back. He has never forgotten that night. Strange what stays with you in Alzheimer's. If only I could have chosen what he would remember and what he would forget.

Friends. They were there for me, providing me with safe ground and acceptance, for which I will be forever grateful. Cami, my chosen sister and teaching colleague, gently filled in where Pat couldn't. Susie, my forever friend, listened, giving me a strength I could draw on. I had no feelings, and yet I had too many feelings. I needed the classroom to forget, to avoid thinking and somehow focus on something else. And yet the moment I was in the classroom, I begged myself to just hang on until the end of the day so I could be alone again. I was a mess.

"Pat, what do I do?" "Cami, what if I always feel this way?" "What if I'm always like this?" I couldn't watch any program that contained a speck of violence, especially the news. Most movies were out. So Pat would bring home Walt Disney videos, and we would laugh. *Cinderella* and *Pinocchio* seemed safe enough. After laughter I would cry, and the cycle would begin again. Pat saw the same tears, the same expressions of pain, the same ups and downs, which seemed to have no end. And so one afternoon I turned to him and said, "Why, Pat? Why do you keep listening to this? Aren't you tired of hearing this same stuff over and over again? You've never told me to get on with it ... I'm not even sure I will ever feel again. What if I don't? When will it become too much for you to take?" Patrick smiled, looked through my pain and whispered, "Hon, that's what it's all about. We're in this together. You would do it for me, right?"

I nodded, knowing that I would.

A Path Toward Strength

I plunged into work. Since everything seemed lost, I had nothing to lose. But there was one thing still there, untouched by all of this. My Spanish. Teaching languages had carried me through other hard times, and now I relied on it as my best ally. I searched for other strengths. In addition to languages, I've always loved to paint and draw. So I began to write, combining words with art illustrations to produce instructional materials for the classroom. First, a series of overhead transparencies complete with classroom instructions and suggested use. Next, I published a tape series designed to help the language teacher reinforce listening skills. Then a book of visual language puzzles to help learn verb tenses, followed by another to strengthen vocabulary. I was on a roll, and with every success I left just a little of the pain behind. To this day, I am still publishing.

And through all of this, Patrick encouraged me. "Keep writing, keep searching outside yourself, do anything that will make you feel better. And if you don't feel strong, look to others. Take their strength to use as your own." When I slipped back into my repetitive despair, he would pull me out. "Strength is inside yourself, Marilynn. It's in there already; you just don't know it."

And as the years passed, I knew it.

Innocence

Patrick adores children, and I have often wondered how very different our lives would have been had we had a family. When we're in church, he inevitably points out every baby in every pew and looks with compassion if they start to cry. I am constantly being nudged when we're in public as he spots a babe in arms or a child walking with his/her parents. And no matter how many times the commercial is shown on TV, he never fails to laugh as he watches a baby sitting on his father's lap reach into a breakfast bowl to eat his father's cereal. He loves their chubbiness, their smiles.

Patrick has no trouble expressing his pleasure and delight. However, this can present a problem, since at this stage of Alzheimer's, social restraints that would have prevented him from expressing himself are gone. He merely reacts.

Recently we were at the mall looking at some DVDs. I was busy looking over the collection, with Patrick nearby. A few feet away, on the other side of him, were a mother and her toddler, whom she held by the hand as he stood by her side. As she reached for a DVD on the shelf in front of her, she momentarily let go of his hand. Patrick, spotting the child, held his arms opened wide, a huge smile on his face, beckoning the child to come to him. The toddler burst into a smile and started waddling over to him, tiny arms held up, taking big goofy steps toward this stranger. When the mother heard Pat calling her baby, she whirled around. I saw the look of concern as she reached over to her baby, who by now was out of her reach, bouncing toward this stranger. I quietly walked toward her, lifted my hand to indicate it was all right, and whispered, "Alzheimer's." The effect was immediate. She understood. I could see her relax as she allowed herself to step back. We smiled at each other. The baby gurgled with pleasure as he clumsily reached the open arms awaiting him. Patrick, lifting the infant in his arms, chuckled with joy and embraced the little one.

Both were laughing, a spontaneous mixture of squeals and joy that was contagious.

Care

Last Friday, carrying books and bags of teaching materials, I was descending the stone staircase in front of a building at the university. In a split second, I felt my foot slide over the next step, and in a desperate attempt to regain my balance I literally ran down the stairs, regaining some balance but losing it again as the speed increased. By the time I reached the bottom steps, it was over. I was sprawled out on the pavement, books and papers flying in the wind, my legs twisted under the weight of my body. In a stunned gesture of denial, I struggled to get to my feet, only to realize they no longer supported me. The pain was incredible. The result of my not-so-graceful descent down the stairs was a badly sprained leg and a cast for the broken bones in my other foot. The entire left side of my body is still a massive black-and-blue mark that testifies to the fact that I will need time to heal.

Caring for Patrick is dependent on my well-being and my ability to meet his needs. These days I'm finding that just getting around is an awkward, if not painful, process, one that does not go unnoticed by Pat. At first he was confused and frightened by my pain. He is trying to help me now with the cast without knowing how. The only thing that he tells me is that I should sleep. It is the only thing he knows. He insists that I go to bed, as if that were the remedy for all known ailments. He can't express himself well, but he becomes agitated, trying to lead me to the bed every chance he gets. The first time, I let him escort me to the bed and then lay there as he tried to tuck me in. I know it gave him the feeling that he was helping, but as he pulled the sheet and blankets over my feet, he tucked them in so tightly I involuntarily cried out in pain. Today I'm faced with the somewhat comical situation of trying to avoid him while completing my tasks of the day without him knowing it. I haven't been successful. Every time I see him, it triggers his nursing instinct and the inevitable procession to the bed.

So this afternoon I will give up. I will ask him to lie down with me, and I will rest—good, wonderful, un-tucked-in rest.

The Phone Call

You don't think that Alzheimer's will ever invade your life. It is, after all, the disease of old uncles and elderly grandparents, of people you don't really know or those you have pitied, slowly shaking your head in empathy. If you ever let the thought creep into your reality, it is probably to confirm that all is well in your world—that all the little slips of memory are just that. That you are still safe …

Alzheimer's came to us through a side door. The phone call came in the middle of the night many years ago. Pat reached for the phone and turned on the light.

Thus began a long journey.

It was my father. He was having hallucinations. He wouldn't go back to sleep for fear the "creatures" would come back, as they had for a couple of nights. He was scared. In his fear and panic, he reached out to his old friend for help. He called Pat. As I lay back in bed, I listened to the comforting words of Patrick calming his friend, my father. Pat assured him that, if need be, he would get on a plane the next morning to be with him. Within minutes there was laughter and the familiar banter that was a part of their friendship. Dad insisted that, no, Pat should not come out. He would be fine. He was just having a couple of bad nights.

Only he wasn't. And so on another night when Dad called again, Pat simply told him to hang on. He would be there.

Patrick flew out to be with Dad. They stayed up all night and talked, a fraternity of two men who loved each other and faced this thing together. I don't know what they talked about. I do know that after that Dad was no longer afraid. Whatever was said between them was enough to carry him through his own battle. My father was diagnosed with Alzheimer's.

When Pat returned, we discussed how this awful disease would someday take away all the memories that he, a friend, and I, a daughter, were part of. Dad had faced the medical verdict with such dignity and strength.

Etched in my memory are Pat's words. I remember so clearly him turning to me and saying, "If ever that were to happen to me … if they don't have a cure, why know?"

Dad

Dad's progression into dementia was a slow process. There would come a time when he could no longer speak, feed himself, or even walk. But for a long time he struggled with speech, trying hard to participate in conversations, and then, at long last, he gave in to silence and passive observation.

I remember a summer late in his disease, when we both flew out to visit him. Two hours after our arrival, we were all sitting around the living room talking. My father, who was sitting in his easy chair observing us, looked at me across the room and asked, "Who is that lady?" He knew my sisters, he knew my mother, but I was a stranger.

My own father didn't know me. Part of me felt that if he just looked at me closer, just heard me talk more, of course he would recognize me. How could he not know me? He had always been proud of me, had always taken visitors on a tour of the house to show off my paintings hanging on the walls. And while I struggled with this rejection, Mom said simply, "That's Marilynn, your daughter." He seemed satisfied with that. There were times during that visit when I'm sure he did know me, but those moments slipped by almost without notice.

On the last day, we were sitting in an area adjoining the kitchen. During a lull in the conversation, Pat walked into the kitchen to heat up a cup of coffee, Dad watching him all the while. As Pat took his mug out of the microwave, Dad's face lit up, and there came a clear, unmistakable "Patrick!" He had finally broken through. Pat gently smiled, "Hi, Gil." Dad smiled back at his old friend before slowly slipping back into his world.

For anyone facing the pain of not being recognized by a loved one; it is not a rejection or denial. It is simply a distance too wide to reach across to take your hand.

Preparation

I received word today that Suzanne, my friend, is going to have her first baby. I could sense her joy and wonderment that this incredible gift is coming. Her excitement was contagious as she wrote of her plans: the little clothes she would buy, the hundred little things she now would look forward to and plan for. She is determined to have everything ready, everything in place, so that her baby will feel safe and well. She is scared and happy at the same time.

I think back to Mom. She had insisted on caring for my father herself. Even with family there, there came a point when she was utterly exhausted and desperate to provide adequate care. And so my father was placed in a nursing home specializing in Alzheimer's. I remember, too, how for three weeks Mom could not bear to be without him, to not care for him. She wanted him home. She wanted him to see walls that were familiar, to eat the food that she always prepared for him. To give him, as long as she could, last things he could hang onto. And so, with the help of home health aides and careful planning, she was able to give that to him.

I now make the choice. For as long as I can, I will care for Patrick at home. It will take preparation and deliberate choices to ensure his needs are met and that I, myself, will be able to meet them. He will be here with me, and there is joy and comfort in that. There is a need to be ready. I think of Suzanne and picture her planning ahead—the drawers of diapers and shelves of powders, lotions, pads, blankets. I, too, have drawers stocked with incontinent pads, disposable gloves, lotions, and ointments. I am determined to have everything ready, everything in place, so that he will feel safe and well. I am scared and happy at the same time.

And so we both prepare.

Time

Time is slowing down. It seems that Patrick has no concept of time or how it relates to daily living. If I try to explain that we have to get going, that we have an appointment, he shows no reaction. If I push to get him ready, he becomes agitated, or, strangely, moves even more slowly. Even when I know we're running late, it is as if he needs to feel that he has all the time in the world.

So I play with time. When we have an appointment, I start two hours early in order to give us the time that he loses. And the strange thing is that Patrick is in some way aware that time is important. Long after he lost the ability to tell time, he still asks me what the hour is, or when we have to be at a certain place. If I tell him the actual time, he goes through the ritual of looking at his watch, even though I know he does not understand what an hour represents. If I do need to tell him about something that will occur later that day, I have to give him a time reference he will understand. Every afternoon Pat watches TV reruns dating from the 50s, 60s, and 70s. He loves them. He can easily relate to when his favorite programs come on. So instead of saying we leave at five o'clock, I say, "We'll leave when *Bonanza* comes on," or "about the time *I Love Lucy* is over." That he understands. And yet his watch is important to him. He puts it on every morning, and it is the first thing he reaches for after his shower. It has some meaning that links him to another time when numbers and hours had their place in his life.

Until today. We were sitting in the doctor's office, waiting. I was very much aware of the lateness of the hour and impatiently looked at my watch. Patrick, too, first looked at his wrist and then touched his watch. For the longest while he studied it, running his fingers over the crystal and then winding it as if it belonged to an era when daily winding was needed. And then he paused, quietly handed it to me, and said, "I don't want this anymore." I accepted his watch.

Once home, I sadly placed it in his drawer, knowing that now it, and time, have been set aside.

The Visit

One of the things you learn very quickly about Alzheimer's is that it changes personalities. In some people it is a dramatic change. In others it is a temporary mood imbalance. I have been fortunate in that Patrick has, for the most part, maintained his cheerfulness. He is basically easy-going, seldom moody or prone to fits of anger.

But not this morning. From the start Patrick was irritable. The breakfast wasn't good. The shower was too cold. He did not want to wear the sweater I laid out for him. To make matters worse, I needed to visit a friend in the hospital and knew that Pat had to come along. The trip in the car was not pleasant. He wanted to know why we couldn't walk and said that he didn't want to go in the car. As we rode through the countryside I tried distraction, always a standby tool. "Look, Hon ... horses!" He looked blankly out the window, then he turned to me and announced that he was hungry. As we pulled up to the hospital, he told me he didn't want to go in, that he would stay in the car. Bribery is wonderful. I would only be a few minutes, promise. And how about stopping off at the diner afterwards, wouldn't he like that?

Having sold his soul for a sandwich and coffee, Patrick turned to me, and together we headed into the hospital. "It's too loud in here! Why do we have to be here?" We had been there five minutes when Pat motioned me over to him and whispered, "Let's get the hell out of here!" With that, he headed for the door. Whoops ... it was evident the visit was definitely over. I raced down the hall as he steadily made his way to whatever corridor he thought led outside. Finally in the car, I sighed at the brevity of my visit and resigned myself to whatever was next. We headed for the diner.

Once there, Patrick was quick to point out that the coffee was awful, and that it was silly to be there since he wasn't hungry. I sat watching him, somewhat fascinated at his behavior. I wasn't paying attention as the waitress approached our table and asked if we wanted more coffee. I smiled and nodded, not realizing that she wasn't pouring decaffeinated into our cups. By the time I caught it, Pat was already drinking coffee, stating that this was a lousy diner and that I had to promise never to come here again. And within twenty minutes I had a different Patrick. He was cheerfully sitting in the car, laughing, excited, pointing out things along the way. "Look … horses!"

The miracle of caffeine.

Clean Shaven

Today he held the shaver in his hand. After glancing in the mirror, he turned to me and inquired, "How much do I shave?" I had long ago replaced his razor with an electric shaver so that Patrick could continue to shave himself every day. I think it important to allow him to participate to some extent in his own care and personal hygiene. I replied as best I could, "Hon, just shave all the new hair so that it all feels smooth, okay?"

It has often been said to be careful what you wish. I would like to add, be careful what you say. After some time I returned to the bathroom to see how he was doing. I stopped in surprise. There he was, shaving, passing the electric shaver over every new hair to make it feel smooth. In addition, on the left side he had shaved his sideburns straight up and over his ears and was in the act of heading further north. A clump of hair was lying on the floor, evidence of his intent. I could only wonder what he would have looked like if I hadn't intervened. I forced myself to hold in a muffled laugh.

He had entered the bathroom with a scrubby beard. And, on the one side at least, he left the bathroom looking unintentionally like a Benedictine monk.

Double Exposure

I thumbed through the photos. They represented a recent outing, and I smiled as I viewed images of Patrick captured as he reacted to moments of laughter and conversation. I handed the pictures to him and watched as he studied each one. He seemed amused, and, when finished, he gently placed them on the table. I went to the bedroom closet, pulled down the box that held our family photos, and put it on the bed. Laying the lid aside, I gathered the new pictures and placed them on top of the pile. I paused. I knew that underneath them were hundreds of photos, all representing past smiles, past years.

My hand reached down to pick some up, but I stopped. No, I would not do this. I would not look toward past times and then be sad as I compared them to the present. I closed the lid of the box and placed it back on the top shelf. Returning to the sunroom, I looked at Pat. He was sitting quietly and smiled as he looked up at me.

My mind flashed back to years ago. I saw him sitting there—whole, healthy—with the same peaceful look, smiling as he looked up from the newspaper he was reading. I stopped.

I had made a conscious effort to not look at photos from the past, and yet my mind had created its own picture. Superimposing itself on the present, memory had created its own image—without my permission—of what Patrick had been in the past. Why does my mind do this? Why does it send my thoughts to former events and feelings when I make a willful intention to stay in the present?

I am finding that this is happening often. A thought or something said can trigger a memory, and in an instant I'm no longer in the present; I have jumped to the past, remembering or thinking about an event distant in time, yet emotionally tied to the present. I know the wisdom of not living or dwelling in the past, yet this is completely involuntary. Perhaps it's my mind's way of trying to come to grips with the present by providing the comfort that memories can bring.

I live with these frequent leaps of thought. They are a part of my life now, somehow blending reality with memory.

A curious fusion of past and present.

The Letter

In the fall of 1994, years before Pat and I realized the true journey ahead of us, we turned on the TV to watch former president Reagan address the nation. From early announcements of his forthcoming speech, we knew he would be talking about something very personal. He had been diagnosed with Alzheimer's.

His words were clear, precise, and came with an effort of character that belied the incredible emotional strain he must have been under. He faced his nation with the dignity that had defined his presidency. He faced this disease with a strength that defined his spirit. It must have been incredibly hard to read that speech. I tried to imagine what he had to be feeling. I could not. He was enduring a private anguish few of us would have to address. But to face this in public was an almost unthinkable trial of courage.

He read the address. He spoke of embarking on this journey through Alzheimer's disease with his beloved Nancy, of wanting to spare her from the pain, but of confidently knowing that somehow she would find the courage to endure. Where was he finding the strength to do this? A trust in God. A trust that his nation would go on beyond his existence to a better future.

Patrick looked at me. He, like me, had been touched by the president's words and the strength it had taken to do this. And quietly he said, "Honey, no one should have to face this. That took guts. Say a prayer for him …"

A prayer that would echo in years to come.

Part II

Early Stages: It Begins

If I knew that tomorrow the world would fall to pieces,
I would still plant my apple tree.

—Martin Luther (1483–1546)

It Begins

I can think of a hundred things that first indicated it was beginning for Patrick. Yet if he weren't sick now, I could point to those very same things as innocent and brush them off as nothing.

Patrick has always loved words. His writing was beautiful, with a sensitivity of expression that was touching. He had an incredible command of the English language, undoubtedly fostered by his training, which permitted him to use nuances of meaning to express himself. Even his sense of humor was tied to words. He always made quick, clever plays on words that could instantly twist a sentence into two meanings, or he'd grab a humorous phrase and run with it. Few people could match his wit.

Sometimes when we were in the car we would have playful conversations in Spanish. He couldn't speak the language, but that didn't stop him. He enjoyed combining the few words he did know with Latin to create his own humorous, if not somewhat ridiculous, dialect. Inevitably these exchanges would end with me laughing at the silliness of it all and the cleverness with which he was able to do it. Not one to be shy, Patrick could also communicate his humor internationally. I distinctly remember the time in Spain when I left him alone at a bistro-type bar while I went to the post office. Upon my return there he was, surrounded by a bunch of Spanish guys reacting and laughing as they all drank *cerveza*. Even the spontaneous verbal games that we loved to create reflected his love for vocabulary. It all came with such ease.

Years later, on one or two occasions Pat stopped mid-sentence and searched for a word. Shortly after that he wrote me a note with three words misspelled. It was curious to me, but nothing more.

Only now does it take on more significance.

Farewell

In one of the many fond memories I have of Patrick as a priest, I hold a strong image of him speaking from the pulpit. In high school I earned extra money working as a church organist on base, often playing for both Protestant and Catholic services. I was able to see first hand his ability to speak. Patrick was humorous. He was human. He used no notes and spoke from the heart. His style was very unlike that of my father, who, in contrast, delivered a polished sermon resulting from hours of writing and revision. A natural, Patrick would walk to the pulpit and begin to speak. His homilies were injected with moments of humor that had the entire congregation laughing, yet within minutes contemplating the serious point he was making.

My father died.

Pat, always the comforter, was there to support me. As always, he handled the flight arrangements and made sure we made connections in Chicago on the flight out West. He was our strength as he held my mother in his arms and gently consoled her. On the phone Mom had asked him if he would deliver the eulogy for Dad, and without hesitation he had agreed. And now, the night before, he was nervous. Perhaps because it was his best friend, perhaps because he hadn't spoken in public for so long, he told me he didn't know if he could do it. I assured him that he would do fine, that if he just thought about Dad, what he meant to all of us, he would find the words. I left him as he worked out what he would say.

The ceremony was beautiful. There was a uniformed escort, and the service was conducted with dignity characteristic of a military funeral. But when Patrick stood up to talk, I knew immediately he was in trouble. He tried to read notes he had written, and failing in that, he stumbled over rambling phrases. I was shocked at his inability to express himself, and my heart went out to him as he tried to cover his embarrassment.

Later he would tell me that he had really tried, but he could not remember what he wanted to say.

Effort

On the flight back home I glanced over at Pat. He had taken out a piece of paper and was writing. I think he was trying to compose a letter to Mom, but halfway through he stopped, crumpled up the paper, and looked out the window. In the following days I would come home to find him at the kitchen table with pad and pencil in front of him, trying to write. I never asked to see what he was writing, fearing that it would embarrass him. There was a kind of silent agreement that if he were having problems, he needed time to find his own way out. Pride is a funny thing. You have to respect it. Everything else was normal. He still read the newspaper every morning, still fixed meals, still joked, still did the hundred things that make life normal. Since retiring from the New York prison system where he worked as counselor/grievance coordinator, Pat had more time for his passion, reading. And there were still times when he helped me write, always searching for the perfect word or phrase.

One afternoon after returning home, I got up the nerve to approach the subject. Would he like me to help? After all, I was a teacher. Perhaps we could find a way to relearn what he had lost. To my surprise, he agreed, and so began our after-school sessions. I created flashcards with multiplication tables; we played number and word games—anything to stimulate learning. In a way I had no comparison, since he was never any good at math, witnessed by the fact that it was I who always balanced the checkbook. He had always admitted that even in pre-seminary days he could never handle math. So our expectations weren't high, and we had a built-in excuse.

But the writing was different. I would come home to find him with yellow note pads filled with rows of words that he had written over and over in an effort to spell them correctly. And strangely, words would still show up wrong in each column. I dictated paragraphs, and as the weeks went by I found myself choosing words I knew he had no difficulty with. I think it was my futile gesture at imparting encouragement. And the strange thing was that, to some extent, he did learn. He was getting slightly better with his multiplication tables and had no problem paraphrasing passages I read. We took any hopeful sign of improvement as proof that this was, indeed, something he could control and improve. We agreed he was aging, that he would be losing some abilities, but that was acceptable. After all, he was coherent; those around him hadn't noticed anything.

It was our little secret.

The Agreement

"Honey, I can't find words. I feel stupid sometimes when I'm talking to others." Because of the circumstances surrounding our marriage, our life had been a very private one. We revolved around each other, and each had always depended on the other. Despite the fact that we always had friends and enjoyed social gatherings, for the most part we were content and happy to be with each other. Now privacy had become a safe refuge. "Not to worry. I'll help you ... I promise. If we're in public and you run into trouble, I'll slip you the word, you'll see." And I kept my word; we developed a strange stereotype-partnership that went unnoticed by others, but which kept the illusion alive. Pat still actively participated in conversations. I, in turn, would listen as he talked and subtly jump in to supply a word here and there when he stumbled. It seemed natural. I noticed that he would do more listening now, laugh more than induce the laughter, but he was not giving up. He has always been a person who has loved humor, and his laughter would cover up any missteps on his part. I'm not sure if people were picking up on this strategy, but even if they were, Patrick himself felt better.

I was surprised how well he could cover. But privately I would try to encourage him to find the words, to not rely on me, to build his own confidence. I simply tried waiting for him to find words, to somehow make his brain work, exercise, recover. It did no good.

We never mentioned the word, but more and more I feared that it might be the beginnings of Alzheimer's. He could not remember things said, and, worse, he didn't understand common words. I'd ask if he could hand me something, and I saw him touching, then pausing over various objects in an attempt to find what I had requested. But I had a promise to keep. If he were afraid of testing, then that was his choice.

Finding Out

I checked with the school nurse. What sort of symptoms were signs of beginning Alzheimer's? What I was learning was confusing. Everyone is different, especially in the beginning stages. I needed to search for a more definitive answer, so I investigated sites on the Internet. When I found a checklist of common symptoms, I plunged into comparisons: *Forgetting things, names*: well, yes, but I've done that, too. *Misplacing things, finding things in unusual places*: maybe car keys, but he had never misplaced things in strange places. *Avoiding people*: no, he could still hold his own socially. *Change in mood or behavior*: no, Pat was still positive, humorous. *Loss of words or forgetting common words*: yes, this was the one. He had some problems, but at this point he could still communicate, and others weren't aware of his struggles. I continued through the checklist of common characteristics, trying to find anything that would say we were safe. Looking back, I can see how desperate I was to try to convince myself that things were still okay. Rationalization is not hard to do. All of us have experienced going into a room to get something only to stand there like a fool trying to remember what we came for. We've all struggled to remember an actor's name or that fourth thing on our grocery list. Gradual memory loss was okay. Maybe this was just a result of his many medications or anxiety. At worst, there was the possibility that he may have suffered from mini-strokes. But the underlining fact was that testing was the only way we would know for sure.

Scared

One afternoon I stayed after school to finish up some work. I came home, walked up the stairs, and there on the landing was a bloody note. On it were scribbled some words … "Not to wory. Hspitl. Sorry blood. I fine."

The shock slammed into my head. I threw my books to the floor, noticing the carpet had what looked like large smears of blood. My heart was beating hard as I got into the car and frantically drove north. Which hospital? Where could he have gone? I tried the first hospital. Nothing. I checked with a nearby walk-in clinic. I tried calling home—nothing. Finally I found the right hospital emergency ward. They remembered him. It seems Patrick had come in to be treated for a bad cut on his hand. And, by the way, he couldn't remember all the insurance information; could I supply it? After giving them the information needed, I got into my car and raced home.

He was fine. Bandaged up, but fine. He immediately apologized for the carpet and said he had tried to scrub it away before he went to the hospital, and that he thought he got it all. He then said he had waited out front for me. I hadn't come. He had waited for me so we could go to the hospital together. When I asked him how long he had waited, he replied that someone stopped and asked if he needed help and told him to get to the hospital right away, which he then did.

I was sick. Patrick had been trying to repair a drawer. With some box cutters, he was cutting cardboard to do whatever he had in mind to fix it. The cutters had slipped and sliced into his left hand. He needed eleven stitches to close the cut. For the first time I was scared. He hadn't taken steps to help himself. He was waiting for me. If someone hadn't come along to advise him, would he have waited out there forever? A hundred things flashed through my mind. Was it time to retire? Should I now be with him? It was becoming evident that he needed guidance. It was the first time I took the idea of retiring seriously.

There is a fine line between helping and creating dependency. I have crossed that line many times. But I am learning. If you take something away too soon, that independent part will be taken away forever. I have much more to learn. I asked Pat if we should consider testing. His face

47

flashed with anger, and he shot back at me, "Why? Do you think I've lost it? Look, if it isn't anything, then I have nothing to worry about. If it is, I don't want to know."

There is a fine line, too, between anger and fear.

Celebration

I retired. It was both a sad and happy decision, but one that I knew eventually had to be made. When you think about all the times you say, "Someday we'll travel; someday we'll put an extension on the house; someday …" This is someday. I don't ever want to look back and say I could have, or, worse, I should have.

In celebration, we took a cruise to Alaska. Cami, her husband Neal, and Mom joined us on a fantastic few days through the Inner Passage. It was a fun time, with incredible food and a chance to relax. Mom got up early in the mornings; Pat preferred to get up late. I was somewhere in between, but the excitement of the trip filled in any schedule gaps. Pat and I would stay up late at the lounge bar comforting a glass of wine while a goofy guy played old songs on the piano and joked with the passengers.

For the most part Patrick did well. At the very beginning he got lost on deck, having tried to return to our cabin as the ship was pulling out of port. He could not find the room number even though he had a marked key and map of the ship. I found him getting off the elevator and saw the look of relief in his eyes as he spotted me. But for the most part he was fine. At this point only Cami knew about what he was going through, and she continually assured me that he seemed fine to her. He had retreated from telling jokes and seemed quieter, but there was so much left of him that it seemed very natural. The fact that he couldn't read well was embarrassing for him, especially at the dinner table. This, however, was solved by simply going to the dining room early, grabbing a menu, and returning to our cabin. There we would sit and rehearse the items on the menu. It gave him a chance to decide what he wanted to order that night. Since he sat by me at the dining table, it was an easy thing for me to order for him if he got in trouble. There were times that he began to shy away from conversation, but if Neal or Mom were puzzled by this, they said nothing.

The Tree

Months later Pat said to me, "You know, Hon, I miss Gil. I really miss him." I knew. I missed my father, too. I often wondered if, wherever he was, he was aware of what his friend was going through. Dad had gone through this. He would understand exactly what Pat was feeling.

On a beautiful summer afternoon, Pat and I decided to attend an outdoor concert held on the grounds of an old estate. We brought along a blanket to sit on and picked out a place far in the back under an old twisted tree. Its shade provided relief from an otherwise warm day. The music was modern jazz played by a trio of talented young men. I watched Pat as he listened to the music. He constantly amazed me. He never complained. He never protested the losses he was experiencing. He was living the best way he knew how. In that moment I was overwhelmed with emotion. I silently said a prayer. Pat was in such need. I asked that if there were a way, some way we may not even understand, a way for Him to even use Dad to maybe reach Pat ... just help him. Pat needed help.

And at that moment, Pat turned to me and said, "This is a pretty tree, isn't it." I looked up and nodded. And then, as if an answered prayer, I saw it. High on the trunk of this gnarled tree was a tiny plaque that identified its species. It read *Gingko*.

We started to read books on health. Among the many books we read, we found one entitled *Your Miracle Brain*. It wrote of dramatic evidence that certain food supplements and vitamins could boost memory and help reverse mental aging. So we added vitamins to his diet. Pat had always taken vitamins, but now there were Ginkgo biloba, folic acid, B12, vitamin E, lipoic acid, niacin, CoQ10 ... even something called phosphatidylserine (PS). He exercised, walked, kept up with our verbal games, and kept writing and reading in an attempt to somehow recover what now seemed out of his reach. And for a while it seemed that Patrick was benefiting from these supplements. Whether real or imagined benefits, Pat felt better taking them. Looking back now, I realize that it was a losing battle, that this disease, at least in our case, could not be affected by anything we did. But in the beginning we had to try.

Books

For as long as I have known Patrick he has loved to read. When he retired, I presented him with the entire collection of his favorite author, Charles Dickens. How he loved the wording and phrasing of this nineteenth-century writer! Many times I would come home to find him sitting back on the couch, book in hand, enjoying the *Pickwick Papers, Sketches by Boz,* or *The Old Curiosity Shop.* He would look up and say, "Hon, listen to this! This guy really knows how to use words … listen how he picks just the right word to describe this character!" He would proceed to read a passage that was filled with such humor and elegance of words that we both would laugh. "Isn't that something? No one can touch this guy!"

Every Christmas Dad and Pat would exchange books, each sending ones they had read throughout the year to share with each other, books ranging from quantum physics to philosophy and psychology. This would be more a journey of searching and learning. Dad would include written passages and notes he had made with questions or thoughts on what he had read. Pat, in turn, would call Dad after reading one of his books, and together they would participate in what could only be called a long-distance book club.

It seemed only natural that we would reach for books to help Patrick as he tried to recover what he thought he was losing. He reached for Dickens, only to be frustrated at not being able to understand what previously had been so easy and enjoyable. So he put those books down. Instead, we included reading together as part of our after-school lessons of flash cards, multiplication, and spelling. I remember picking *To Kill a Mockingbird* to read, not only because it was a favorite, but because it had extensive dialogue that we could enact, Pat taking one role, I the other. Together we would read out loud, then discuss what we had read, with me helping with any words that seem to puzzle him.

And now, with all that behind us, we still read. Every day we sit down, take out a book, and read. Only now it is I who read to him. It is a quiet time that speaks volumes for the beauty of words and his love of reading. And while now the books are simple, with passages I sometimes skip over because he won't understand, he still loves the sounds of phrases and the soothing fact that we are sharing this together.

And I know that someday we will have to put these books down, too.

The List

We had always shared household chores. When one couldn't get to the store, the other would grab the shopping list and stop on the way home from work. As we worked on improving reading and writing, I started to incorporate a shopping list as a way to exercise these skills. It seemed a natural way to increase his ability to recognize difficult words. He would have to read from the list and search within the store as he looked for brand names and food shelves. So in addition to the daily requirements of bread and milk, I started adding less common food items in an effort to help him gain confidence: *soy sauce, mayonnaise, Jell-O.*

I knew that Patrick enjoyed this task. It gave him a chance to interact with people while serving a useful purpose. He had always loved to converse, and now he could enjoy the social contact of striking up conversations with fellow shoppers.

And it seemed to be working. Patrick would come home with his bag of groceries and place the food on the counter. When asked how he was managing, he simply smiled and said, "Great. No problem." So, pleased and encouraged, I began to add even harder items to the list: *balsamic vinegar, nonfat evaporated milk, hazelnut flavored decaffeinated coffee.* And each time the results were positive.

Once I was in the store checking on an item at the customer service desk. As I was talking to the store manager, I mentioned that in the future my husband might be coming in, that he sometimes had trouble with reading, and that once in awhile he may need some help deciphering something on the shopping list. I described him physically and was interrupted—"Oh ... you mean Patrick?" I looked at her. "He comes in here all the time. He's so funny!" She smiled as she continued. "He used to just ask what an item was, where to find it, etc. But I think he's got us wrapped around his finger! The last few times he's just handed us his list!" With that she turned to a fellow worker who was coming down the aisle. "Marcie ... this is Patrick's wife!" There was an immediate response. "You're Pat's wife? He's a riot!"

So that's how he did it ...

The Walk

Walking has always been one of our favorite pastimes. So many memories were forged while walking, talking, and commenting on things around us. Now with more time, we walked more. I think walking gave both of us a chance to unwind and simply share time together. When I was unable to join him, Patrick would take brisk impromptu walks that always ended with his comments on the fresh air and his renewed energy.

I don't remember him leaving the house that afternoon. I was busy inside doing odd chores. I became aware that he had been gone for some time but gave it little thought. In reality, I was relieved that I had not joined him. It was a hot afternoon, and I was content to be inside, cooled by the air conditioner.

And then it became late. I looked outside and realized that it was long past the time for a normal walk to have ended. Should I go search for him? Would it embarrass him? I remembered that once he had been returning home from upstate and had gotten lost. A routine trip that normally took two and a half hours had taken him nearly five. That was last year. And now he had been in the heat for too long. I got into the car. As I searched the streets of our town, I finally saw him. He was walking in the right direction, toward our house, but his gait was uneven, labored. He seemed disoriented and was unaware of me as I pulled up beside him.

Pat climbed into the car. I asked if he was all right, and then asked if he had become lost. He said nothing, merely nodding his head. Within seconds the cool air revived him, and we returned home. I knew it was the last time he would walk alone.

Facing It

I had kept my promise as long as I could. There came a point when I knew that promise had to end. He was having trouble. He no longer could hide his inabilities from others. It was apparent within seconds of a conversation that he was incapable of normal dialogue. He seemed lost. If medications could at least slow down the process, then I had to open that door for him. During this period Dr. Valow, his personal physician, did so much to help me. She was aware of Patrick's condition and sensitive to my dilemma. What she helped me see during consequent visits was that maybe my reluctance to have him tested might have stemmed, in part at least, from my own fears. She didn't push, but rather gently guided me toward help through medication. She had given me time to decide, and I now knew the time had come.

Before the exam, I privately asked the neurologist, Dr. Jaeger, if he would somehow help me keep my promise by not mentioning the word "Alzheimer's" to Pat. He looked at me and said that if Patrick were to ask him straight out, he would have to tell him the truth. I nodded. The testing began.

At first he simply asked Pat why he thought he was here. Patrick, invoking humor, teasingly pointed to me and said, "Her." There were thirty questions: what month were we in, what was his favorite baseball team when he was growing up, could he count backward from one hundred by sevens? At times Pat seemed confused and unable to understand. When Dr. Jaeger handed him a paragraph to read, Patrick merely said, "I don't do that anymore." He kept looking at me to help him, puzzled that I wasn't. Once, he gave an answer and looked hopefully to the doctor for confirmation. "Am I right?" The doctor said nothing and waited for a further response. For a second Patrick seemed confused, so I quietly said, "Honey, he knows you're having trouble and just wants to see how much, so maybe he can find a medicine to help you, okay?" And, mercifully, Patrick never asked the question I was dreading.

In the hallway afterwards, I spoke again to Dr. Jaeger. He gave me the results; Patrick was having trouble with speech and could not express himself. I already knew that. He had lost reasoning power and short-term memory. I already knew that. He had missed twenty-nine of the thirty questions. He had Alzheimer's.

I already knew.

Acceptance

When I returned to the room, Pat was standing by the window looking out. Down below a young boy was running in circles in the snow, a golden retriever chasing him. I quietly walked up behind him, and, with my arm on his shoulder, we watched together. I couldn't speak. It was several moments before I whispered, "Come on, Honey. Let's get something to eat, okay?" He turned to me, and, as if he had never come to this place, he smiled and nodded.

I cannot answer those who may ask why, or how, I could break a promise I had made. If the judgment of that action overrides the benefit of medicines that may or may not help him, then I have to live with that. It is a small price to pay for the greater pain of not trying to help him. That afternoon Pat's life seemed to go on as usual. We ate. We talked. We stopped by the store on the way home.

We never mentioned this day again.

Language

We have invented our own language. And like the games we used to play, we use anything to make ourselves understood. Only now it isn't a game. It is real.

In late afternoon as the sun is going down, he will hold his arms wide and say, "Can you make it big in here?" I know he wants me to turn the lights on. Sometimes the words come out funny, sometimes not at all. And Pat laughs—at first a chuckle, which will turn into genuine joviality. It is so natural to choose laughter. We will laugh at the ridiculousness of it all, at the fact that we are trying so hard and sometimes failing so miserably. Pat will be the first to laugh, his eyes crinkling the way I always loved. "Honey, I'd like ... you know, red, good water ... please?" And I will go to the kitchen and return and hand the Italian his daily glass of red wine.

Until later stages, the lack of words has never prevented us from communicating. Perhaps because I teach languages, I am used to people being frustrated at not being able to express themselves. It has always been a challenge to me to help them find a way to say something in the simplest of terms, using words they do know to express something they don't. This is no different. Eventually I know that I'll be the one who will try more than he to understand. He takes for granted that I will always understand him. His world depends upon that. This pseudo-linguistics is a way of creating the illusion that he can communicate better than he does.

And illusion works just fine.

Music

Today he was restless. No matter what I did or said, he could not be calmed. Quietly talking with him produced an acknowledgement but did little to relieve the anxiety that he was feeling. Patrick was always such an easy-going being, rarely becoming upset. Maybe in all those years he simply hid his feelings, and now, with no mask to hide behind, fears that have long been held in check bound to the surface in uncontrolled expression.

I had seen this before. It was the last summer of Dad's life, and we had flown out to Seattle to share what little time was left. Mom and Pat had gone to the store, and I was left with Dad, with instructions to try to keep him away from the "books." In the deep stages of Alzheimer's, Dad had become obsessed with finances, investments, etc. No longer able to understand what had once been a pleasurable pastime, the stock market had now, for him, become a curse. Dad would ponder over the monthly statements, dutifully kept in a financial book. Over and over he would desperately try to figure out where mistakes were, if financial collapse was eminent, what the final sum of money was. I placed the book in a separate place, thinking maybe he would forget what he was looking for. But that only added to his frustration, so in the end I was forced to hand over the one thing that both eased his anxiety and cruelly fed his fears. He searched pages in a vain attempt to understand, while I stood there perplexed and helpless. If only I could distract him.

Dad and I have always loved music. In his youth, in a romantic gesture of feeling for my mother, he had even composed a song for her. It held the wildly romantic title of *Night of Ecstasy*. I started to hum the melody, and, as if bewitched by music, he stopped and listened. Then he smiled, gently put the book down, and began to hum. I could reach him through music! And so that afternoon I sat with my father and quietly began to hum hymns. He hummed along, contented with this rare touch with reality. Pat came across the scene and left, only to return again, quietly taking pictures with a camera. A gift to me, to forever remember this moment.

And so now I sat at my piano and played for Pat. And like his friend before him, he sat back and quietly listened.

57

The Bird

I was sitting in the front room reading. I heard a loud thud against the front picture window, and I looked up. Nothing. So I turned back to my pages. But something was different. A sound of loud chirping broke my train of thought, and I once again looked up. It was coming from the large evergreen tree standing close to the house, in front of the window. There in the branches was a brilliant red bird, hopping from limb to limb calling out. I was fascinated. Had he crashed into the window and was now screaming his pain? Why wasn't he flying away? And then it dawned on me. I quietly stepped to the front door and ever so slightly opened it. He saw me and immediately fluttered away, only to fly back again to a higher branch and begin again his chorus of wild calls. I ventured out on the front steps and looked over to the front window. There, clinging to the edge of the windowsill, was another bird. Her dull-colored feathers gave away the fact that she was his mate. She was alive, but the blow of crashing into the window had left her stunned. She was facing inward toward the house and could not be seen from inside. It was evident that she was in shock. I quietly closed the door and went to get Pat.

When we returned to the front room, the red bird was still there. He was still calling out, wilding moving from branch to branch in a vain effort to help her. I pointed to the bird, and Patrick stared at the beauty of this bright red cardinal. For several minutes we stood in our living room, watching as the male remained in the tree.

I pointed to him. "See, Honey? See how he never leaves her side? He won't leave her. He knows she's hurt, but he will stay with her until she can fly away with him." I took his hand and said, "That's us, Patrick. I will never leave your side…promise." He nodded. We watched as the cardinal kept hopping from branch to branch, the sounds of encouragement coming loud and clear.

Part III

Middle Stages: Living in the Now

I am not afraid of tomorrow, for I have seen yesterday and I love today.

—William Allen White (American journalist, 1868–1944)

The Elevator

This afternoon we went to a doctor's appointment. As we were waiting for the elevator, a gentleman approached without Patrick being aware. Pat turned and accidentally bumped into him. Instinctively and without hesitation, he said, "Excuse me." The stranger smiled and mutually excused himself. With that, the man stared at the panel above to see whether the elevator was descending and then said something. Patrick responded with a one-word acknowledgement. As the elevator doors opened, the man started talking, and Pat followed him into the elevator, conversation continuing. This was a perfect pairing—a man who loved to talk and a man who needed to listen. Pat was contributing in the only way he could, a word here and there, accompanied by intent listening. And encouraged by Pat's verbal responses and smiles, the man launched into a litany of observations and descriptive narrative, occasionally looking at Pat as he talked about this and that. As long as Patrick didn't say more than three words and looked at the gentleman, things went fine. Pat chuckled, then laughed, not really understanding but reacting to the man's laughter. I, in turn, stared straight ahead, watching the floor indicator lights on the panel, hoping that this innocent scene would go on forever. I smiled. The man didn't know.

And when the doors opened at the floor where the man would get off, the two men parted, shaking hands as they separated. One left the elevator content that he had imparted his thoughts to a willing audience.

And in the elevator, the other was content to have been part of a normal conversation.

Through His Eyes

For the last two weeks I haven't been able to wear makeup due to some minor surgery I had on one eye. While I would like to think the difference in my appearance hasn't been that great, reality has a way of revealing itself. Today, once again cosmetically in place, I felt comfortable and back to my old self. Pat was sitting on the sofa, and as I entered the room he looked at me. He stared for a second, then smiled. "Pretty!" And then he said, "Come here." He reached out his hand, and as I leaned down he touched my face and asked, "Is that you?" I started to laugh. Well, yes, it was me. And then he repeated, "You're pretty!" And despite the fact that makeup was the deciding factor here, I accepted the compliment. In his honesty and simplicity, Patrick had noticed me. Somewhere inside I felt like a school girl again.

He's aware of me. He still thinks I'm pretty.

The Long Good-bye

Today I am sad. He had been a student of mine, returning to college from his home after Thanksgiving. He was driving in the rain and was somehow hit by another car. He died hours later in the hospital, having never regained consciousness. He was only twenty-one years old.

Keith had learned German on his own so that he could fulfill a bargain made with his grandfather; if he learned the language, they would travel together in search of family roots in Germany. He was talented in music, a natural athlete, gifted in languages. He had a sense of humor that could catch me in a second and a smile that was both playful and inviting. Nearing high school graduation, he had won a prestigious award sponsored by the Brookhaven Laboratory on Long Island and was invited to bring a teacher with him. And though at that time he had chosen a career in something other than Spanish, he had honored me by naming me as the teacher who had influenced his life. I was touched. I sat with his parents, who, so proud of their son, smiled at seeing this young man's life begin.

And now this. I was stunned at the news. How can a young life with so much potential be taken away so quickly? Somehow Pat's long descent and its inevitable end seems fair compared to the injustice of a life ended too young. My heart went out to his family. And then it came to me. In Pat's illness I have been given a great gift. If someone were to knock on the door and tell me there had been an accident, I would have asked why I couldn't have had just a little more time to say a thousand things to him. And I have been given that time.

Time to let go little by little, until finally I can learn to let go completely.

Progression

When you're dealing with dementia, you begin to realize the importance of routine. We take for granted the daily things we do that create stability in our lives. But for someone who is losing his grasp on reality, security is based on continuity—trusting that what has always been will be there in the future. Patrick depends on routine.

Every morning is the same. We get up; I test his blood sugar. Pat is diabetic. Rather than pills or shots, we are able to control the disease through diet. So taking his blood sugar in the morning gives me a clue as to which type of breakfast I will fix, carbohydrates or proteins. He is no longer able to take the blood samples himself but only rarely protests to my doing so. Following this, we head for the kitchen sink, where we wash his hair before heading for the bathroom to shower and shave. Forget trying to save time. I have found that if I skip a step for one morning, he becomes concerned and tries to tell me what is missing. So the ritual continues. Up until now, he has been able to dress himself, and he made it very clear that he wanted it that way. But the last couple of days I have noticed that he will look at his undershirt. He knows that something has to go over his head, but he cannot figure out how to accomplish this. Unless I step in, he will remain staring at his clothing in a vain effort to figure out how it is done.

Last February Patrick was sick. It started off as a slight cough, which became progressively worse over the weeks. In fact, when I brought him in, he already had a bad case of bronchitis. Pat has asthma, and the doctor asked if he had been taking his medicine. I am very careful about his medications and have made sure I watch Pat as he takes his inhaler morning and night. But as it turns out, for the last couple of months he hasn't gotten the medicine into his lungs. It never dawned on me that, yes, he was using his inhaler, but he had lost the rhythm of inhaling. He had been simply spraying it into his mouth. But I am learning that there are inventions for everything. Now we use something called a "spacer" that allows me to spray the medicine into a chamber. Pat can then inhale it at his own pace.

And so, one by one, the signs are given to you that it is, indeed, slowly progressing.

Necessity

We were traveling up north, sailing along in the car listening to a favorite CD. It became evident, however, that I would have to make a pit stop, and soon. At home it had been simple (well, relatively so). I could help him in the bathroom. In public was a different matter. What was I to do? It's one thing to bring a child into the restroom with you, but a grown man?

I stopped at a rest stop along the interstate and walked up to the security guy standing there. "Excuse me, my husband has Alzheimer's and will need my help in the restroom. Should I go into the woman's or men's restroom with him?" He looked around, temporarily indecisive. The need was imminent now, so I made the decision. I simply said, "I'm going to announce I'm bringing him into the men's room, okay?" He said that would be fine.

I gingerly opened the door. "Ahem … excuse me, guys, I have my husband who has Alzheimer's with me, and he needs to come in. Is it going to bother anyone if we both come in?" No response. Okay— deep breath, here we go. I entered with Pat, looking straight ahead, not letting my eyes shift to the right as we walked past the urinals and into a booth. This was a first for me. How the heck do you get two people, one of them in haste, into a tiny booth? Very carefully. Shutting the door was in itself a problem, with coats, purse, etc. But after awhile our voices echoed in what seemed to be an empty restroom. Relief. Good; walking out would be easier if there weren't many guys out there. After what seemed like an eternity, we finally exited the booth. Hand cleaning was prolonged by the fact that Pat was disconcerted by the hot-air hand dryers. I sighed as he insisted on doing it over and over until every speck of moisture on his hands was gone. Then, as we exited the restroom, I noticed what could only be appreciated by anyone who has waited in line at Disney World. The security man was standing in front of a long, winding line of waiting men. In an overly generous attempt to help, he had held up all the male rest-stop visitors in order for us to have privacy. I slowly walked past the line of men waiting with various degrees of self-control, apologizing for making them wait.

I vowed that next time I'd try the women's room.

The Car

If anything dominated Pat's attention, it was our cars. Though he was not mechanical, he maintained both vehicles with a thoroughness that approached pit-stop quality. Tire rotations, oil changes, yearly check-ups, inspection stickers, maintenance—all were handled with a dedication of purpose that left me on the sidelines, quite willing to concede this activity to him. He gave attention to every detail. Even washing the cars was a ritual in which I did not participate. My style allowed for gaps of unwashed metal, and I preferred to leave the fussy care to him.

He was a better driver than I. He shook his head at the numerous fender dents and scratches I produced, though he never rebuked me. He seemed to accept my less-dedicated approach to driving. When he drove, however, he was in charge. If I forgot to put my seat belt on, he'd stop the car and firmly reach over to pull it across me. "Precious cargo," was all he used to say. When I drove I was more—or less—in charge. He was observant of my mannerisms; if, as often was the case, I wildly gestured while emphasizing a point in our conversation, he would capture my arm in mid-air and move it back to the steering wheel. The silent message was loud and clear—both hands on the wheel.

I worried about how and when Pat would give up driving. For a long while, his reflexes and reactions were good, but his inability to read signs eroded his confidence. As time went by, it became evident that his driving life was coming to an end. I think Pat knew this, and never protested when I walked to the driver's side. "Hon, do you want to drive?" I would always ask first. "No. Why don't you this time?" would always be his reply. This ritual continued until the time when he simply walked to the passenger side of the car and got in.

Last night we washed his car and took it for a final ride. Today we removed the *For Sale* sign from the window, handed the keys to a stranger, and then watched as the new owner backed the car out of the driveway. I watched with interest as Pat's car slowly disappeared down the street. Pat watched with indifference, barely reacting, then turned his attention to a squirrel that was running across the yard.

Comparison

You cannot approach this disease with a game plan. That has been one of the hardest things for me to learn. I have always been a person who thinks ahead, who always plans, in an effort to anticipate a disappointment before it happens. But this thing is cruel. It makes its own rules, and if you try to substitute your own, it will very soon teach you that you can't.

I find myself thinking about Dad. I find myself measuring him. Where he was at this point, how much loss he had, and—the one milestone I don't want to face—how much time he had left. And so I now look to Mom as someone who has gone through this before me. She knows and has experienced the pain I have yet to face. I remember once watching her gently work with Dad—bathing him, feeding him, handling all the personal things you don't want to imagine. How could she handle it all? When I addressed the question to her, she simply said, "You don't have to handle it all. It doesn't happen all at once. Little by little new things are added. You can always add one new thing." And it made sense. If you can handle just three things, a fourth thing later on isn't so bad. Just don't think of the ten things you'll eventually juggle. The wisdom of my mother.

I have a little plaque that I keep in a place where I will see it every day. It has carried me through a lot. It reads:

COURAGE

Doesn't always roar.

Sometimes courage is a quiet voice

at the end of the day saying:

"I will try again tomorrow."

The Treasure

Today I had to leave the room and walk into the kitchen. A big lump came to my throat, and if I had stayed I would have cried.

Pat had wanted to wrap my Christmas gift. I laid out the paper, scissors, tape, etc., and indicated to him that he could use anything he saw to wrap my gift. A kind of quiet determination etched itself on his face as he confronted what must have been a confusion of paper, bows, and ribbon. I returned to washing dishes, humming along to the CD of Christmas songs in the background and letting my thoughts float back to childhood memories, a time of snow, fruitcakes, and Bing Crosby. After what seemed to be the longest time, I returned to the bedroom and smiled as I saw that, despite minor flaws, he had done pretty well at wrapping the gift. The smile on his face proved that he was pleased. Undoubtedly encouraged by this success, he then said he wanted to write my name on a gift card, but he couldn't remember how to spell it. I carefully wrote my name in huge letters on paper so he could copy it. Then I left, leaving him with pen and card to face the task at hand.

I was in the other room when he finally came back to show me the results and to ask if it was right. Even with my model, he had gotten most of the letters wrong, but I told him it was just fine. He had spent so much time to do something for me. I was touched. And then, unexpectedly, he looked at me with such sadness. Slowly he shook his head and said that he was sorry he couldn't do anything anymore.

My Patrick was sad. I just held him, and we rocked back and forth. The Christmas music was still playing, and I felt this great love. I love him so much it hurts. After a few moments I left him to gather up his treasure to place under the tree. I returned to the kitchen with the same sadness he was feeling, but with a strange happiness as well. I said a prayer to thank Him that He had made it crystal clear that I had needed to retire. I know that I never would have had these moments with Pat otherwise. We are happy.

Pain

In the middle of the night I could hear that Patrick was in distress. He was yelling in pain, and even before I reached him I knew what it was. His legs had cramped up, and he was bewildered by the pain. "Mom, stop the pain! Mom!" I reached him just as he was trying to get up, and he threw me aside in a feeble attempt to somehow turn off the pain. He kept yelling, "Mom! Do something!" I was trying my best, saying, "I'm here … I'm here," but he could find no comfort in my words. What should I do? I tried to get him on his feet, to get his circulation going. No good. He kept pushing me away. Heat. Try heat. He couldn't stay still. He struck out at me. There was no way I could lessen the pain. Massage his legs. He yelled out even more. I was helpless. Finally, mercifully, the pain took its own course, lessening according to its own rules. Patrick, breathless and exhausted, sat on the edge of the bed rubbing his knotted legs.

And I, assigned the role of mother, could only sit next to him and tell him everything was okay.

Night and Day

I always thought that once someone with Alzheimer's forgets something, that knowledge is gone forever. But there seems to be a stage when inconsistency plays a major role. I can ask Pat a question about something, and he hesitates and struggles with vague recognition. Yet, curiously, I can ask that same question three weeks later, and he will have total recognition and make an appropriate response. There are days when he seems in control of logic and perception. At those times people have said to me, "But he seems pretty good to me," not knowing that eight hours prior Pat didn't know where he was or who he was talking to. They think what I used to think—that Alzheimer's destroys, leaves its mark, and then boldly moves on to the next undamaged area of cognition.

What goes unnoticed until you live with the disease awhile is that there appear to be times when it lessens, fading into false retreat, only to come back to take more. Nights and early mornings seem to be the hardest for Patrick. He struggles with awareness, often trying to figure out where he is and what people's names are. On two occasions, he has looked at me through stranger's eyes. Yet in the afternoon he's clear enough to settle into a routine and actively participate in conversation. Dad was different. He experienced what has been labeled as *sundowning*—a confusion that increases as the afternoon continues. Why the difference, I do not know.

But I suspect that this will not always be. There may come a time when there is no difference between morning and night, a week or a month. And that consistent behavior will be the proof of greater loss.

Mirror Image

We were staying at Cami's house for the weekend. It was a joyous occasion, celebrating the birthday of her husband, Neal. The surprise party had been a complete success. With us in the house were Neal's brother and his wife, Anne, who suffers from the late stages of Alzheimer's. "What's that?" Patrick asked me when I mentioned her condition. I replied, "You know … like Dad." He looked sad and sighed, "Ahhhh. That poor lady."

The evening was late, and we were tired as we settled into our bed for a long night's sleep. Somewhere in the night, Anne had become restless and disoriented. Unknown to her husband or to me, she quietly slipped out of their bedroom and came into ours. By the time I was aware of the situation, Anne was trying to climb into bed with Patrick. I had to refrain myself from laughing at the humor of this unexpected ménage a trois. Patrick shot up out of bed and stared at her, blurting out, "What the—who are you?" And for a moment the poor lady looked with blank eyes at Patrick who, in turn, stared at her. At that moment, I intervened and said as gently as I could, "Anne, you are in the wrong bedroom. Go back now to the other room, okay?"

I led her to the appropriate room and left her as she entered their bedroom. When I returned to our room, Patrick turned to me and asked, "Who was that? and I replied, "That's Anne. She has Alzheimer's. She didn't know what she was doing. It's all right. Go back to sleep." And Patrick sighed,

"Ahhhh. That poor lady."

The Gift

For ten minutes I had him back. For ten incredible minutes he was clear and articulate, the words coming effortlessly. For ten minutes he was the man I always knew: caring, witty, and funny, wanting to take care of me. I was hungry for every word, every thought he was so clearly able to express. I absorbed each second for myself. I listened as he talked, not daring to think of when it would end.

What do you say to him in those ten minutes? What do you tell him that he can take with him when he goes away again?

Lilies

I had been going over boxes of papers and sorting out files when I found the old article. It mentioned Father Patrick Garzione, the church he and his family attended, and a brief summary of Pat's high school and seminary education. The church. I remember Pat mentioning this church in the past, but in all those years I had never seen it. So one afternoon I knew I had to find it.

Last Sunday we went to the church of his youth. As we entered and then slowly walked down the aisle to a center pew, I watched for any sign that he remembered something so permanent, so significant, from his past. But there was nothing.

Here Pat was baptized and served as an altar boy. I remember Pat once told me of a particular Easter Sunday long ago. He described the church as being filled with lilies and potted palms, arranged in front of the altar and crowded along the railing and altar steps. He described it as a jungle of Easter lilies. He was the lead altar boy, whose duty it was to lead the other altar boys up the aisle to their assigned places up front. The processional hymn began, and young Patrick proceeded up the aisle, where he soon found himself faced with all those lilies. Instead of going the prescribed route, Pat took a shortcut, leading the procession in and between the branches and palms, pushing branches aside and crawling through the plants and over the pots of lilies to the front. (He also described a stern lecture that followed the Mass.) I smiled.

I looked around. The sound of the organ echoed off the marble pillars. How many times he must have heard this same organ, seen these marble pillars, looked up to these stained glass windows! Pat gave his first Mass here as a young priest. All of this was a part of him.

I will always hold this place as special.

Advice

"Mom, you've got to find some time for yourself. Promise me you'll give yourself a break sometimes." I remember so clearly expressing concern for the fact that my mother was with Dad twenty-four hours a day without a break. I tried to tell her how important it was for caregivers to give themselves time alone, away from responsibilities.

Funny how different it is when you're the caregiver. So now it's my turn. And, just like my mother, I hear myself saying, "I'm fine, really. I'll be all right. Don't worry." But when it comes right down to it, caregiving is hard. You think you'll be able to handle it all, one day at a time. And for a while it works.

Once I was watching a program on TV. There was a brief scene on board a plane when flight attendants were explaining emergency procedures. *In the event of a sudden loss of cabin pressure, air bags will automatically drop. Place them firmly on your face and breathe in normally. Those with small children or persons unable to care for themselves should first place their own mask on before helping others with theirs.* It made sense. In order to fully help others, I had to first help myself.

For years I had used my spare time to teach classes at the State University of New York/ Language Immersion Institute at New Paltz. Now teaching became a lifeline for me as I struggled to schedule time for myself. The classroom had always been my joy and had now become a chance to come out of myself and into the lives of others.

And so I was able to leave Pat and teach. As long as I prepared meals for him, as long as I called him every few hours, he was fine. At this stage he could not read numbers, and changing TV channels presented a problem. So I simply put every TV on in the house and called him when it was time to move into the next room for his favorite programs. Later, when I no longer could leave him alone, I was able to have a qualified caregiver look after him in my absence.

I am not a morning person, but I force myself out of bed early each morning so that I can have that time for myself. It is my time—time to do something, or do nothing. Time for a shower, time to sip my coffee, to read, to write … to think. I have found that by refreshing my body and mind I can, indeed, take one day at a time.

The Moment

I woke up this morning to find the house freezing—the thermostat registered in the low 50s. It was evident that the furnace had gone out during the night, and the day promised to be a cold one. My first impulse was to pull the warm covers over me and deny the whole thing, but reality called for a more practical approach. So I gingerly stepped on the cold floor and made my way to the back room. It dawned on me that the little gas fireplace in that room would give Pat a warm place to dress and stay while we waited for the "furnace guys" to come.

With the phone call made and the fireplace started, I hurried to the kitchen, where I flipped the on-switch to the coffee maker, prepared the night before. (Funny how sometimes survival is as simple as a hot cup of coffee.) After a few minutes the back room was at a tolerable temperature, and it was time to awaken Patrick. He was not helping the situation. Moving at a snail's pace and protesting taking his meds, Pat seemed to reject any notion of having his blood sugar tested, taking his asthma inhaler, dressing, etc. I find that whenever things go awry and upset his routine, he can't handle it and begins to protest in slow motion. I, in turn, go into my adjusting mode and very rarely give in to other thoughts.

But that was my mistake. While Pat was constantly complaining that his nose was running, saying he wasn't going to sit down to breakfast, I was trying to put long johns on him in an attempt to keep him warm. And while I was holding his clothes trying to get him to put them on, I let my mind fall back to how he was, how this wasn't what I, or he, had bargained for ... and I blew it. I blurted out, "Honey, every time I try to help you, you make me wait, you won't help me out! Why? ... Why won't you help me? Sometimes I feel like my entire day is spent waiting on you and you like it that way! I can't take this!"

And at that moment he looked at me. And then, slowly, he reached out and put his arms around me. As if he were still the comforter, he tried in his own way to console me. At that moment I buried my head in his chest and rocked in his arms, pretending it was as in years before when he would dry my tears, holding me close. And then, as I let him hold me, I locked this moment in my mind for the times in the future when he won't be able to comfort me.

The Other

There were two Pats. One was in the next room. The other was in my mind: whole, healthy. And for a moment I chose between the two. I wanted the other Pat. I wanted the Pat in my mind, my memories. I could feel him as if he were real. If I let myself, I could easily have imaginary conversations with him. I could easily be in the car, in the store, pretending that he was with me, humoring me, commenting on things throughout the day. That was the real Pat. That was the man I wanted. This man was different. It wasn't him. How dare he replace my Pat! My Patrick is healthy. He might only be out for a while. He would return. He would walk through the door with a joke, a smile. He would dance rings around me with logic. He would be miles ahead of me in thought and reasoning. He would be strong.

I was rejecting him. Stop it, Marilynn. How could you have these feelings? And what have you gained? You will end up just where you started, and then what? He needs you. He is real. He's in the other room waiting for you and your help, your comfort. He's waiting for you to be with him. Do you really want to turn away from this Pat?

I felt awful.

Cost

I turned from the kitchen counter and walked over to the table, coffeepot in hand. I looked at my friend and smiled, thankful that we had these few minutes together. She had a way of knowing just when I needed her company, and today in particular I was enjoying our time together. After filling her cup and then mine, I sat down, placing the remaining coffee on the table rather than getting up to return it to the coffee maker. I took a deep breath and turned to speak. She had been watching me.

"Marilynn, you look tired. I can see that this is affecting you. It's costing you a lot."

She was right, of course. But I think that in any relationship—whether characterized by sickness or health—that is true. There is always a price tag. Love is going to cost. It is going to cost in giving. It is going to cost emotionally, and sometimes it will hurt. It is going to cost in time and in moments of pain and frustration.

And then you think about it. Like everything else, you make choices. You consider the price and how much you have to spend. And if you have ever loved, you reach down into your pocket and understand that, despite the cost, it is worth it.

Simplicity

I have found that as things slow down, there emerges a simplicity that is remarkable. There are no longer big needs, big explanations, big anything. Everything is reduced to small pleasures and simple times.

On a late summer afternoon Pat and I went to see the balloons. They were gigantic, bright, beautiful. They rose gracefully into the air borne by warm air currents, and they made a whishing sound as gas heaters were lit to produce the hot air. It was an incredible display of color and form. Balloon rides were being offered to the public, but there was no way that Pat would be able to tolerate that. It didn't matter. We stood there in awe of the beauty that was unfolding above us. We said nothing. After awhile I glanced over to Pat. He was looking up, and on his face there was an expression of such peace and contentment. And like that afternoon so long ago when I sat with my father humming hymns, I had the need to remember this moment.

I reached for my camera.

Need

There was a time when it was Pat who protected and cared for me. I remember a particular day years ago when I had a bad headache and wasn't feeling well. I had a slight fever. Pat was leaving to go upstate and left me with instructions: "If this thing gets worse, I want you to promise me to go to a doctor, okay?" And throughout the next few hours he would call, asking if I was feeling any better. He was always overly protective of me, and so I assured him that everything was fine. Then in the middle of that night I awoke to an incredible pain in my chest. With every breath I took, the searing pain would cut into me so that I was scared to take the next one. I couldn't catch my breath, and when I tried, it came out in gasps of astonishing pain.

Looking back, I realize that I should have called the hospital immediately. But I didn't. Instead I called Pat to ask his advice. Upon hearing my gasping voice, he screamed at me to get off the phone and call an ambulance. A fog was overtaking me and I think it was he who called the ambulance.

The next hours and days are a blur. This was the very week that Jim Henson, the creator of the Muppets, had died of an aggressive form of pneumonia. I entered the hospital with a temperature of 105.9, courtesy, it turned out, of the same deadly bacteria that took Henson's life a few days before. I was placed in the ICU. Ice blankets covered me to bring down the fever. I was hooked up to tubes and given antibiotics and painkillers. I was delirious, struggling between bouts of confusion and fever. I kept thinking I saw Patrick's face close to me, and then I would slip back into a fitful nothingness. I remember waking once to the beep-beep of some monitor and seeing him there. His face was drawn, and he whispered, "I can't lose you, Marilynn. You are a part of me ... please." I was too weak to respond and could only close my eyes. I vaguely knew there was something he wanted me to do, but I couldn't put the thoughts together. Every time I woke up, he was there telling me, "Sleep, Honey. Not to worry. I'm here."

I slept. And every day I woke to see him there. I remained in the intensive care unit for nearly a week, followed by another seven days in a hospital room. In the weeks of home recovery I felt safe and protected, comforted in knowing that Patrick was there to care for me. I needed him.

I always have.

Closeness

There are things I miss. Often in the process of providing home care, something personal is lost. Sometimes I have the need to again be protected by him, to depend on him, to be cared for. I miss him holding me. I miss his warmth, his touch.

In a moment of defiance, I decided that I would not give that over to this disease. It would not rob us of everything. So this afternoon I simply asked if he would put his arms around me. He has always loved to hold me. We sat close together, holding each other. And since he couldn't say things to me, I began to say things to him. I told him of times long forgotten; I told him of things we used to laugh at, things we loved to do. Patrick listened, smiling as I told him how we first met, how we first knew we cared for each other. I told him of when we were married, of how the next morning we got up early and took a walk together in the snow.

And then as he has done a thousand times in a thousand moments in the past, he touched my face and said, "You're my girl, aren't you…" I smiled and nodded. Yes.

Chocolate

On a beautiful day we decided to go to Mohonk, a mountain resort located outside the town of New Paltz, New York. It's always been a special place to relax, walk around the lake, and enjoy the turn-of-the-century edifice with its creaky wooden floors and fantastic views. In addition to its resort atmosphere, Mohonk is noted for its food. On this particular day, we decided to stay for the lunch setting—a fantastic buffet that always offers a rich variety of foods and desserts.

"Patrick, look at all this food! Isn't it incredible? It's a buffet. You can have anything you want to eat!" Pat looked in disbelief. "I can have anything?" I smiled and nodded as I began to fill up my plate. Pat, following my lead, loaded up his plate until there was a mound of roast beef, ham, salad, pasta, and baked bread. As we were taking our plates to the table, we passed the dessert buffet. I tried to walk by rather quickly, because Patrick is diabetic, and I would rather not have to limit his choices. Patrick loves chocolate, and as we passed by I could see him eyeing the impressive variety of cheesecakes, pies, chocolate cakes, tarts, and puddings.

The meal met all expectations. I was stuffed, but Pat said he would like some more. Seeing that he had done just fine dishing up by himself the first time, I pointed to the buffet and said, "Hon, why don't you go back and get some more ... in this place you can have anything you want!"

I watched, making sure he arrived at the buffet table. Then my attention switched to the waitress, who had just arrived at our table to see if we wanted another drink. The pin she was wearing caught my eye, and together we admired its sparkle and rattled on about where she had gotten it. Our pleasant conversation ended abruptly as Patrick returned to our table. I saw a shocked look on her face and turned just as Patrick exclaimed, "Here, this is what I want ..."

...and he placed on the table an entire chocolate cake.

Fun

Our fun has always been simple. It has come more from discovery and spontaneity than from planning. Half of Pat's fun was seeing if he could thwart my attempts at ignoring his humor. He enjoyed my surprise and my fake indignity and especially the fact that he could always find a way to crack me up.

There was the time we decided to make cookies together, each competing to come up with the best design. I carefully filled my cookie sheet with gingerbread stars, half moons, and delicate streaking comets. Patrick presented me with his tray of anatomically correct gingerbread men.

Fun sometimes came in an instant of whimsical decision. On a summer day we watched a small town parade, standing on the sidewalk with other people as the band marched by. Behind it came a large group of local people carrying a huge banner dedicated to community pride. They marched by, waving and smiling at the applauding crowd. In an instant Patrick smiled, then grabbed my arm. Within seconds we were a part of the parade, blending into the group, waving and nodding to people as we passed by.

And now, though in simplified form, he still seeks fun. This morning I was washing dishes, he was drying. As the phone rang, I grabbed the end of his towel to wipe my hands. In an instant Pat seized the moment, grabbing my hand as he watched me reaching for the phone with the other. Only when he saw me stretched to ridiculous lengths did he chuckle and let go. His laugh told me he is still having fun.

The Seagull

Today I was driving when a squirrel darted across the road. Instinctively I glanced in the rearview mirror before putting on the brakes.

I remember years ago I had been driving, with Pat seated next to me. Up ahead on the road was a group of blackbirds feeding on a recently killed squirrel. Immediately I slammed on the brakes and then heard the screeching of cars in back of me. "You can't do that!" Pat admonished. "Look, there are always cars behind you. You've got to make a decision. If a squirrel, a bird, whatever, is on the road, you can't stop like that. You've got to use your head. And anyway, birds are smart. They'll get out of the way." Months later I was driving and spotted a lone seagull feeding in the middle of the road. Pat's words echoed in my mind, "Not to worry—they'll get out of the way. Keep driving."

I did. It didn't.

I came home in tears. The second Pat saw my distress he was there, sitting me down and handing me the towel he had been holding. When I told him I had had an accident, he immediately asked if I was all right. Through sobs I managed to convey, "It was awful! … .the car … I …" He interjected, "Forget the damned car—are you ok?" Once convinced that I was unhurt, he waited for me to gain some composure. I tried to speak. "I was driving and it … it … I hit …" I couldn't bring myself to say it. He gently encouraged me. "Take your time. You're okay. Now, just tell me." Through my tears I looked into his eyes and found there a pool of comfort and solace. With great emotional effort I finally mouthed the words. "I hit … I hit a seagull."

He stared at me. And then this face—this face of endless compassion and understanding—began to transform. Slowly, almost imperceptibly, the corners of his mouth started to curl upward. He struggled to hold it in, tightening his lip in an effort to maintain a look of concern. For a moment he managed, but then, unable to control it any longer, he gave in to a muffled sound and finally burst out laughing.

He ducked as I threw the towel at him.

Friends

I don't think Pat knows how much he is loved. Friends who were always there are still here. They feel the painful truth that Patrick is slowly losing his grip on reality. But they are hanging on for him. They write to me. They remain in the background, keeping up with how he is doing. They come to visit. And even though I know it must be painful for them to see him like this, they do not shy away. Bryan brings his dog, Mr. Peabody, and Patrick laughs at the antics of his playful Scottie dog. Frank continues to send Pat articles relating to a time when they were both priests, long after knowing that he can no longer read or understand their significance. It is simply a message that he is still a part of life, of what is. He is included in conversations for what little, or nothing, he is able to contribute.

And his friends encourage me. They speak to me of how Patrick helped them in the past. They tell me of the countless times he had them doubled over in laughter. He had been a true friend who always accepted them for what they were, no strings attached. And so now they accept him. He is still that friend, damaged in body but not in spirit. There is no need to be anything other than what Pat is. He is loved.

Writing

We have always celebrated Three Kings Day. Having each lived in Puerto Rico, and both loving the Hispanic culture, we took joy in celebrating the arrival of the Magi to Bethlehem, on the January 6th Epiphany.

We never gave each other many gifts. At Christmas we chose to give one gift rather than a flood of presents. On Three Kings Day we would then give each other three small gifts, each one reflecting something we created rather than bought. One year I created a nativity scene, complete with little figures that I sewed and stuffed. Another year I presented him with an appliqué blanket that I worked on every chance I had, waiting impatiently for the moments when he would leave the apartment.

But Pat's gift was always writing. Each year I would look forward to an original story that he would write. I knew it was coming. He would ask me for a title, saying that he would then create a story around that title. I took joy in trying to find the most obscure, ridiculous title I could think of ... "He Never Had a Chance," or "A Broken Fragment of Green." Sure enough, I would open my gift to find a story created just for me. Each was written with such clarity of thought and sentiment that I never ceased to be amazed at his ability.

I loved when he wrote to and for me. I kept even the letters of our early correspondence, which had been filled with guidance, comfort, humor, and tenderness. I knew, too, that he had kept all my letters. But when together we decided to separate to allow him to reaffirm his vow of celibacy, he had told me he was going to destroy those correspondences and anything that reminded him of me. I had nodded in agreement. I, however, did not discard the letters he had written to me. I vowed to myself that I would live without him, but if I needed strength in the years ahead, I could turn to them for comfort.

And I still have them. They are tucked away in a secret place. I cannot read them now. Maybe someday, when the pain lessens and I need his strength, I may reach for them. But not now.

Released to the Angels

It was the last time Pat attempted to write. He came to me one morning, long after we had abandoned our learning sessions, asking if we could try again to see if he could write. My heart was breaking as he spoke, knowing that this, too, would fail. But he was reaching out, trying to hang on. I nodded, and together we went to the table to write. I put the paper in front of him, and as he took the pen he asked if he could try this alone. I quietly left him as he tried once more.

I don't remember much more about that session, only that it was the last. And this morning I came across that piece of paper. I couldn't throw it away. I wanted to understand what he so desperately had wanted to say, knowing it was the last thing he ever wrote. It took me nearly fifteen minutes to unscramble what he had put on paper. Words were misspelled to the extent that you had to try for the whole sentence before, little by little, the pieces fell in place to reveal what he was trying to say.

And then it came through. Sentences of thought, locked behind a mind that no longer obeyed his will. I put the fragmented pieces of words together and found that he was, in fact, expressing himself. Without the misspellings, without the fragments that were merely scribbles, it read:

"There is no reason to make believe that everything is ok ... it isn't! ... I do not know what I am doing. Why? Because I do not have the ability to find out what the hell I do on a piece of paper. The ability to record your thoughts ... I cannot make sense in this ... (a) problem which is either a joke or penance that can only be a chance to pray for people who are asking God to be released ... purgatory ... to be released to the angels. I am hopeful that my help will find others ... to help those who cannot believe that God loves them. The fact is that if one calls forth, (He) will take them into His arms."

It was evident that even in the anguish of what he was going through, he still reached out to God.

Once a Priest

In all the years we were married, Patrick maintained his spiritual faith. Our marriage had meant that he was excommunicated from the Catholic Church and could not participate in the Sacraments. Yet I knew he longed to have that a part of his life, too.

It was made so clear to me one afternoon many years ago. Pat came home, and the instant I saw him I knew something had happened. His pants were covered with mud, and his face was solemn, white. I immediately asked if he was okay. He nodded but said nothing. He went to the fridge, poured himself a glass of wine, then went into the other room and quietly closed the door. I felt shut out, worried. I stood by the closed door and asked if everything was all right, but he said he needed to be by himself for a while.

In a few minutes I heard the door open, and he came over to me. He apologized for shutting me out and took me over to the couch and sat me down. He then told me what had happened. He had left our apartment after a light rain shower to take one of his long walks on the road outside the complex where we lived. Up ahead he saw an accident that had just occurred. The police and ambulance hadn't arrived yet and he had run to the scene to help in any way he could. There he found a woman lying on the ground in a pool of water by the side of the road. She had just been hit by a car. The driver of the car was walking around with his hands on his head screaming he hadn't seen her walking. Pat immediately went over to her and knelt down. She was obviously dying. He stayed with her, and in the minutes before the ambulance arrived, he prayed with her. Pat said she held his hand and was able to mouth the words as they prayed together. She died before help arrived. Pat looked at me with tears in his eyes, and I knew this had been hard on him. He had been a priest for over twenty years. That would always be a part of him. It was something locked so deep inside I would never be able to touch or fully understand those feelings.

In the years that followed, we talked about the possibility of applying for laicization, the process whereby a priest could be released from his vows and return to the level of parishioner. The process was complicated and long, requiring the approval of the Archdiocese of New York and the Vatican in Rome. It was something that only Pat could decide to do. He knew I would support any decision he made.

Petition

Once when I was going through some closets and drawers in an effort to simplify and clean, I came upon a thick notebook of paper, discolored from age. I looked inside to find pages that Pat had begun to write. It was written years ago, long before the onset of Alzheimer's. Addressed to the Tribunal, it was a summary of his life, his intentions, and his reasons for asking to be released from his priestly vows. It was not complete. Judging from the many times he had started, the many crossed-out phrases as well as entire paragraphs, it was evident that he was struggling with what he would say and had abandoned his attempt. I didn't want to read more. I closed the notebook, knowing that this was private and belonged to him.

I had always believed that the reason he hadn't applied for laicization was his easygoing nature, in which procrastination sometimes played a role. So often I would smile at him for his ability to do things *mañana*, and whenever I would inquire, "Hon, have you gotten around to this/that yet?" he would smile and invariably reply, "Sure, almost finished. I'd say tomorrow we're looking at the finished product." He would chuckle and I would laugh, knowing this was a game between us. But this was different. The fact that I now knew that he had started so many times makes me believe that it had more to do with a personal struggle than anything else.

His intention was clear. And so, when it was evident that he was losing ground with speech and writing, I once again approached the subject. This time he looked at me and said, "Yes, I really want this. Honey, will you help me?" I had never helped him with writing and in all honesty, had no idea how. Once a letter of petition had been sent to the Tribunal of the Archdiocese of New York, we awaited a response. Pages of questions and uncompleted forms came. So the first step was to let him try again. Time after time, page after page, he tried. Nothing would come. So it occurred to me to conduct a taped interview of the questions and answers so he could more easily express his ideas, which could then be summarized on paper. This worked well, and although Patrick stumbled over words, he was able to express clearly his history, his inner struggles, his need to be reconciled with the Church. I then revised and transcribed the recording into written form. I read it back to Pat, and he made corrections, inserting more statements as we went along. He was satisfied.

The Process

Few people make an inspiring impression on you that lasts. One such person is Monsignor Vella. He attended the same seminary as Pat and was two years younger. He now worked as the head of the Metropolitan Tribunal of the Archdiocese of New York, in charge of handling petitions for laicization. When we started the process, he was the one who reached out to help us. He would write letters, helping us with the technicalities and informing us how the petition was proceeding. On one particular phone call, I was able to tell him of Pat's difficulty and growing losses. He was understanding and worked even harder to bring this about.

When Pat and I decided to marry, we were well aware of the impact this would have on his family. We fully understood and accepted any rejection on their part. One of his four sisters embraced her brother in acceptance. Through the years I have grown to love Joan, and it was to her that I now turned for help. She, along with two wonderfully dear cousins, wrote letters that accompanied the petition on its way to Rome. We then had to go to New York City, where Pat was to conduct his personal interview with the Tribunal. He was nervous on the train going into the city, fully aware of the importance of this trip. Once there, we were greeted by Monsignor Vella. I felt immediate relief. He gently spoke to Pat and guided him to where they would conduct the interview. I remained in the outer office, waiting. Within minutes, Monsignor Vella appeared and asked if I would come in. Pat was having difficulties, and the Monsignor felt it would help him if I were there with him. The interview, however difficult, was over. Afterwards, the Monsignor graciously sent us a copy of the proceedings so that we would have time to review and edit it before he sent it to the Vatican.

We prayed. This was something that Patrick wanted and needed. We prayed for the strength to accept whatever the outcome. And so it was that after months of waiting, I came home one afternoon to find a letter in the mailbox. Pat's request for laicization had been granted by the Holy See.

Peace

Patrick was reconciled with his Church. He could now participate in the Mass and receive Communion. He was at peace.

As this disease progresses, I have found that I have to rely more and more on what I know *was*, in order to make complete what is *now*. It is now up to me to help him follow rituals and prayers he no longer remembers. We go to Mass and I wait as he takes Communion. It makes me happy to watch him as he walks up the aisle to partake in what I know is meaningful and essential to his spirit. During Lent, Joan, his sister, fills me in on what my Protestant upbringing did not teach me, so that Patrick can once again fast and participate. It was important to him in the past, and so I make it important now. It is as it should be.

Long ago Patrick and I had agreed that if he were ever laicized, we would then be married in the Church. This choice was not a denial of the legitimacy of our first marriage. It was rather an acknowledgment that our union would be witnessed, too, by the Church. Again I turned to Monsignor Vella, and, true to his generous nature, he agreed to marry us.

On a cold winter morning we gathered at his church on 14th Street in Manhattan. Cami and Neal were there with us to act as witnesses. As Monsignor Vella asked Patrick to repeat after him, Patrick spoke the vows he had given me twenty-eight years before. And then, because no one had asked him to stop, Pat continued reciting my vows as well. The four of us smiled, not wanting to interrupt this innocent moment. When Monsignor Vella asked me if I would love and cherish him, *in sickness and in health*, I paused. All the love I have ever felt for this man filled me, and I heard myself saying, "To love and cherish in health … and in sickness."

It was Christmas Eve.

Hope

No matter what I am doing, either the radio or television has always provided a comforting background sound, whether I am conscious of its content or not. Today Patrick was filling some freezer bags with leftover lasagna and seemed content with the chore given him. I, in turn, was putting dishes away and wiping countertops, part of the normal routine of after-dinner cleanup. I was vaguely listening to the program going on in the other room, not really focusing on its content, yet aware that it was concerned with common health issues. A doctor was being interviewed about his experiences with new medicines, and in the course of time the subject turned to Alzheimer's.

At first I paid little attention. Over time I have become immune to the description of this disease and its effect on victim and family. I shy away from the impersonal portrayal of something so personal. Yet as the interview continued, talk turned to new approaches to and treatments for the disease. I walked into the other room, dish in hand, watching as the doctor described new treatments being offered in Europe. He expressed the hope that soon experimental drugs would be available in America. He was enthusiastic as he expressed his convictions that soon there would be a way to detect the beginning symptoms long before word loss and memory problems take over and that, with the development of these new medicines, this disease could very well be wiped out in years to come.

Hope. Enthusiasm. I looked back at Patrick sitting at the kitchen table and felt no joy, no hope. This joy and enthusiasm belong to others. They will walk out of the doctor's office with relief. They will feel the immense gratitude that a medicine has been discovered that will make things better. Their hurt will go away. I am a realist. I know that no matter how long it takes or how soon it comes, he will be left out. It will be too late for Patrick.

Better Than Nada

I could hear him in the other room calling for me. Not quite sure if this was a call of distress or a simple invitation to join him, I dropped what I was doing.

When I got there he was smiling. I relaxed. Patrick was eagerly pointing to the TV screen and looking at me to respond. On the television the movie *Tin Cup* had just come on; credits were playing, and the lead melody was unfolding. There on the screen a lazy armadillo was walking across the highway to the catchy beat of *A Little Bit is Better Than Nada*. Pat was caught in the song's rhythm, moving his hands and smiling. I couldn't help but join him in the rhythm of this country western song.

I turned the music up. On an impulse I grabbed him and pulled him to the center of the room. We laughed. The happy rhythm invited us to react, and so we both twirled in a homemade, Tex-Mex sort of way. Patrick loved it. So did I.

♪

A little bit is better than nada,
Sometimes you want the whole enchilada,
A little bit is better than nada,
A little bit or nothin' at all.
♫

We had it. The whole enchilada.

Again

We met each other through business. She was my editor, who worked with me through the process of publishing an educational CD-Rom I created. In time, I found out that Julie's mother was facing a possible diagnosis of Alzheimer's.

Alzheimer's is not a rare disease. The chance is great that you will encounter others who are also about to face this. And when you do, it's as if you are suddenly facing it all over again. Feelings come to the surface. You remember the horrible conflict of wanting to know, while fearing how you will handle and accept it once you do. You struggle with keeping things normal, and in some ways you try to accept this thing long before you confirm that it is true. You cling to hope. The emotional battle is debilitating.

Julie is aware that the upcoming tests could very well reveal that their mother suffers from the disease. She is concerned for her sister in Vermont, who is with her parents and cares for them on a daily basis. Since Julie lives and works in Michigan, I fear that distance may cause feelings of guilt for not being able to help her sister or comfort her mother and dad.

I know what lies ahead for them. I wish for now that I could alleviate the anxiety associated with diagnosis for Julie and her family. I know that I cannot. I know that at this point nothing—no amount of encouragement or concern—can take away what they are about to face together. I feel sadness for them.

I think back. Is this what Mom felt when she first heard about Pat?

The Request

Of all the daily routines, Pat loves when I wash his hair. Maybe it's the sensation of warm water, of massaging his head. Maybe it's feeling me close. I don't know. There is no way I can attempt to save time by bypassing this event. When I'm running late, it doesn't matter. He will point to his head, and I know what he wants. Even the time when I accidentally forgot to use baby shampoo and stinging suds got into his eyes, he didn't complain. It didn't deter him from enjoying this daily ritual the next time.

This morning I washed his hair at the kitchen sink. Then I brought him to the bathroom mirror and handed him his comb. I came back some minutes later to see him standing quietly, staring at himself in the mirror. It must have been one of those rare moments when he looked at his appearance. Patrick has kept his dark hair all these years, and although it has thinned somewhat with the passage of time, there are only a few strands of gray above, accented by more silver in his beard. He turned to me and with trusting innocence asked, "… can you get me some more hair?"

I had always met his needs and requests. This, however, was testing the limits of my capacities as a provider.

The Lesson

I was scrubbing floors in the kitchen. I never thought I would reach a point where I love the daily chores of living. I think, to some extent, my world has slowed down. Once my life was filled with lesson plans, meetings, deadlines—all things that needed to be addressed and never permitted me to enjoy the now. I'm learning to slow down. I have to. The now is too big. I'm beginning to find "my time" in the little things I do and am enjoying it. In years past, whenever I was upset about finishing something so that I could get on to the next thing, Pat always told me, "The monks used to say, 'When you wash the dishes, wash the dishes.'" It had nothing to do with the dishes. It had everything to do with concentrating on the task at hand and doing that to the best of your ability, without worrying about what was coming next. Good advice.

The trouble with advice is that sometimes the very person who gives it has a way of interrupting its effect. There I was, hands in hot water, doing my own version of wax-on, wax-off meditation when Patrick walked into the kitchen. His world no longer concerns itself with consequences. He walked over my clean wet floors and stood looking at me. His face was happy. "Come … come." There was an urgency in his voice, but his face revealed an absence of concern. With no need to worry, I relaxed. Not thrilled at the interruption, I sighed as I put my rag down and heard my bones creak in an effort to accommodate my rising body.

He took my hand and led me to the living room. There, in the middle of the room, he spread his arms wide and made a complete circle to encompass the entire room. What? What did he want me to see? I looked around. Nothing. Yet the joy on his face was evident. I looked again. Nothing. I was missing something.

And then, as if he were teaching me a new version of enjoying the now, I looked harder. The afternoon sun had filled the room. It was bouncing off the cream walls, echoing on the carpet, ceiling, furniture. The room was bright, calm, beautiful. And Pat stood there mesmerized, joyful in the light. We stood there in the bright afternoon, soaking in the treasure he had found. He was content, happy to share his joy with me.

Part IV

Advanced Stages: Letting Go

... joy can spring like a flower even from the cliffs of despair.

—Ann Morrow Lindbergh (1906–2001)

Enough

Accepting loss is a slow, aching process. But it is real, and as it unfolds, the process creates its own learning. I have found that in our life together Pat and I have become incredibly close because of pain—something we hadn't planned on sharing, but which has let us reach out to each other. I look at our life together. I know if he's here, I can make it. I'm not sure about the strength needed for next week or next month, but for right now I know we can do this together. No way do I want to think about future moments. They will come soon enough.

When I think about the past times that have been meaningful, it dawns on me that the moments I remember most were not spectacular. They were simple moments. And so I look at right now, at this very moment, and I know that things are good. And that's it. That's enough.

I am learning. He is teaching me. Through his impatience I am guided toward patience. Through his pain, I am learning empathy for others out there who must be in pain. I am learning that things will never be near the perfection we want, but that there is joy in imperfection.

He was looking out the window. I was working on some lesson plans for a class I was teaching, and as I stood up to leave the room he reached out to me. "Stay..." was all he said.

So I stayed.

Playing

I had gotten up to enjoy the early hour by myself. But even as I sat relaxing, I found that this morning I wanted to be with him. So I quietly went to the room and slipped into bed with him. He was lying on his side with his back to me, so I snuggled up behind him, wrapping my arms around him and feeling his warmth. I listened to him breathing. His asthma was clearly having an effect. As he slowly breathed in and out, I could hear an after-effect from his lungs—a whiney, wheezy sound that lingered on far after each breath ended.

I rested my head on his back and listened. The slow, rhythmic sounds of his breathing continued. And then, the strange whines started coming in groups. I listened. *Weeeee—wo-wo—weezzzzii.* The groups were now becoming varied: ... long ... short, short, short, long ... short.

He was playing. He was well aware that I was with him, and he was controlling the sounds of his own breathing. He was holding on to the bottom of each breath so that the exhaled sound produced a strange mixture of mini-wheezes followed by a long, tiny, animal-like whine. I nudged him. It stopped. Then after a few seconds, it quietly began again—*wee, eiouuu, weezzzzuuuu.* I smiled as I heard what sounded like a tiny chipmunk being squeezed. I nudged him again. It stopped, but not before he took delight in sneaking in a couple more chipmunk wheezes. He waited a couple of breaths, then, teasingly, he began again, continuing with long exhales in the hopes that I would again nudge him to stop.

The chipmunk sounds kept coming—cute, short, mournful little whines. I giggled. And then, knowing that he had made me laugh, Patrick began to chuckle, shaking under the covers as he silently enjoyed the effects of his breathing.

Midnight Run

Finding time has become a major issue. It seems ironic that I retired in order to have more time to be with Patrick and now, while I do have more time, it is becoming filled with increasing numbers of tasks and activities needed to care for him. He still can be left alone for very short periods of time, but I can see that soon this will end as his dependency on me increases. His care begins in the morning and doesn't end at night. He is now beginning to get up at night, confused. I gently make sure he is all right, escort him to the bathroom, and then head back to bed. It seems to be all he needs for the moment. He lets me tuck him back under the covers, and I know that for a couple of hours at least, he will go back to sleep.

If I need time for grocery shopping, I have to search for it. At one time I brought him with me every time I needed to go to the nearby store for milk or bread. But that becomes a problem when he's not feeling well or is reluctant to go along. So last night I tried out a plan. In the wee hours of the morning, Patrick needed to get up. After staying with him and making sure he went back to sleep, I quietly put on my coat, jumped into the car, and headed for a supermarket in the nearby town that is open all night.

What a wonderful discovery! The store was virtually empty. I felt excited as I grabbed a shopping cart and headed for the produce section. The whole experience of shopping at that hour with no one around was fantastic! There I was, rolling the cart down the aisle, quickly checking off items from my list and humming along with the music quietly playing throughout the store. No trouble finding a parking space, no line at the cash register. It was perfection.

And then I headed home. I slipped back into the quiet house and placed the dairy products and vegetables in the fridge, leaving the other bags of groceries on the counter to empty in the morning. I crawled back into bed with a smile, knowing my midnight run to the store had been a complete success.

The Music Box

I smiled as I handed him the box. I knew he wouldn't know what it was or remember the fact that it was he who had given it to me years ago.

I remember the first time I opened it. It was years before we were married, an occasion unmarked by celebration or event. He had simply handed it to me and smiled. "It's for you." It was a gesture that spoke of genuine affection for me on his part, yet still respectful of the boundaries we both had chosen to place between us. I remember reaching for his gift and then slowly, carefully, lifting the lid. The soft, melodious sounds of the music box filled me with joy and the wonderment of expressed emotion. I smiled as I looked up at him. "Do you like it?" he asked. I was absorbed in the delicate melody—the simplicity of quiet notes that, when combined with each other, created a joyful expression. I looked back down at the box. He had chosen this for me. He had given this joy to me. I tried to answer his question but found no words. I simply nodded.

Today I carefully took the music box from the shelf. Pat was sitting in the sunroom and I sat down beside him. I said quietly, "Here, Pat. This is for you." He reached for the box and gently placed it on his lap. "What is it?" he asked as he looked curiously at the simple box while his hand moved over the polished wood surface. I smiled, "Open it…"

And then, as he lifted the lid of the music box, a twinkling of notes filled the room. For a second he was startled at the sound and stared at me. Then his eyes filled with wonder as he looked down at the source of music and then up again at me. He smiled. "Do you like it?" I asked. Again he looked at the small offering of harmonic joy. He found no words.

He simply nodded.

Energy

Patrick has always had energy. The idea was always stuck in the back of my mind that as years went by Pat, being older than I, would gradually lose mobility and would have a hard time keeping up with me. Not so. He was always the one who had more than enough energy to discover and enjoy events of the day. Whenever we traveled, it was Pat who searched for things to do, always finding interesting things for us to see and urging me to join him in experiencing the flavor of local events. I think back to days off from work when I was perfectly content to stay at home, lounge around, and enjoy the luxury of recuperation. Not the Italian. He was always off in his car, leaving a message that he'd be back soon, then returning home with bags of groceries or announcing a plan for what we would do later that day. The mornings were always the same: the sound of the electric shaver, the somewhat irritating singing in the shower followed by bright, perky greetings of the new day. I, on the other hand, am not a morning person and consider coffee to be more than a beverage. For me it is very close to salvation. I think he took pleasure in my sleepy-eyed approach to a new day, and I suspect he often initiated conversation simply to enjoy my reaction. It was his smile that gave him away.

Last night I was constantly getting up. Patrick was confused and needed to be talked to, guided back to bed, and convinced to go back to sleep. I lost count after six times. I only remember falling into bed the last time in an exhausted resignation of strength and consciousness. This morning I'm exhausted. Completely, utterly exhausted. And Pat came to me. Bright, perky, happy. Ready to start the day.

I looked at him in wonder. Some things never change.

Omnipotence

I'm a perfectionist who has in no way achieved any state of perfection. I've always set goals, sometimes unrealistic, and then relentlessly worked toward them. In the past, success has often been outweighed by moments of frustration and failure as I struggled with limitations. And always there was Pat and his gentle counsel: "Listen, Marilynn, you're way too demanding of yourself. Keep trying, but there's no way you're going to be perfect. Imperfection will always exist. Hey, ya got to remember—there was only one guy who could walk on water."

Today the overcast sky gave way to torrents of rain that pounded the windows and roof of the sunroom. Pat stood looking out, in awe of the downpour. After several displays of lightning and thunder, he paused. At that moment a spectacular flash lit the sky. He turned. "Tell it to stop," he said as the deafening thunder muted his words. Surprised that I did nothing, he repeated, "You'll make it go away, right?" The mental image of me commanding the wind and rain to obey my voice made me smile.

Either he had revised his theory, or I had gone up a notch on his scale of acquired perfection.

Perspective

I am constantly reminded of what others see. When I mention that my husband has Alzheimer's, there is always an instant reaction, most often empathy and inevitable sympathy for the situation. I marvel at that. They don't see what I see. I know that others must feel a slight awkwardness, which comes from being sensitive to how I will react. Many times they take cues from me. My openness invites their openness. I am touched by that.

Was I like that? Did I, at one time, see only the sadness and horribleness of Alzheimer's? I can't remember. I do remember that, as a child, I was afraid of older people. I saw only the oldness: the wrinkled face, the awkward walking, the confusion of senility. If someone were to gently explain that this person had been someone far different, that even now there were endearing things about them, I probably wouldn't have said anything but would have thought differently. There was an uneasiness, a fear, on my part. It was something I had to experience.

I realize that people must see a far different Patrick than I do. They don't see that, yes, all the miserable things that we hear about Alzheimer's, all of that is true. But there is also a gentleness, a collection of countless good things that are never talked about. If they could have seen Pat as a young man, a mature man, an older man, complete with experiences, humor, acceptance of life and people—they would have a fraction of what I see now. They would know that this shell isn't just the leftovers of a man.

It is not fair of me to demand that others see that, too. If they read the anecdotes I write and then see Pat as he is today, they could very well be disappointed with what they see. No doubt they would have built up in their minds a picture of a man whose appearance would, or should, somewhat reflect the stories of his past. That image would be quite different from the frailty that time and disease have created. But he is all those things to me.

It is just a matter of perspective.

Loss

Today I got word that Pat's old friend died. Joe was his buddy from the seminary who, like Patrick, had left the priesthood. Over the years they had kept in touch, getting together to laugh, share a drink, and talk. Joe would call to keep Pat up to date on the news of fellow classmates and how they were doing. Pat would often go into the city to stay the weekend with Joe—two ol' buddies sharing good times together. Now I pondered how I could bring myself to tell him. How would he handle this, knowing he was one step closer to being alone?

I picked a quiet time and sat down beside him. "Hon, I have some bad news to tell you … I got a letter today that says that … that Joe died." He turned his head and searched my eyes. "Who?" My heart sank. One by one the layers are being peeled away, but not this. I was stunned. He could not remember. And Dad … when would he not be able to remember Dad? And when would it be my turn? I clung to hope. "You remember Joe. He was your friend who was in the seminary with you. He was the one who …" I stopped. Why was I trying to make him remember his friend? So he could then feel and remember pain? So that he could pull back memories that would make him sad? It was *I* who still needed him to remember. It was *I* who was feeling the loss. Pat was, at last, immune. So I simply said, "He was a friend who died … but he's all right now." Pat quietly nodded and sat back.

And inside I heard myself pray, "Let go, Marilynn…let go."

Ease

I found the large envelope tucked away among some boxes in the attic. In it were photos, military medals, awards Pat earned while stationed in Formosa and in Vietnam. *Medal of Merit, Air Force Commendation Medal, Meritorious Service Award . . .* He had never referred to these, had never once made mention of how they were earned. I quietly placed the medals back in the envelope. He had not wanted to be measured by these. He had simply wanted to be Patrick.

Pat was always a guy's kind of guy. He felt at home sharing a beer, telling jokes, or simply enjoying the company of others. There were no pretenses, no expectations. I think, to some extent, this down-to-earth quality contributed to his effectiveness as a priest; he was human, nonjudgmental, accessible.

Humor. Whether in the company of an elderly lady or with a group of truck drivers, he was at ease, setting a humorous tone that generated smiles and laughter. He was often sarcastic, but always with a kindheartedness that never sought to hurt. His comments stemmed from an openness that accepted others as they were, yet did not permit anyone to step over personal boundaries.

It wasn't put on. It was genuine. He hated outward show and could tell phoniness a mile off. He felt uncomfortable with titles, and though highly educated, he shied away from any mention of degrees or academic standing. Ease came on the personal level—an enjoyment of the now, independent of past action or proof of achievement. That ease is still here. Now deficient in the skills necessary to generate verbal humor, he still reacts to it, sharing in the laughter and good-naturedness of those around him.

He is simply a man content to be in the presence of all things created equal.

Stillness

As we pulled into the church parking lot to attend the regular Saturday five o'clock Mass, I didn't give much thought to the fact that there were no cars. Knowing that it was Easter weekend, we had arrived early, and so I reasoned that we had made it to the church ahead of the crowd. Then as we entered the vestibule, I saw the posted sign. I had forgotten. The Easter vigil service was to be held that evening at eight o'clock instead of the regular hour. I turned to Pat, who was still climbing the stairs, and told him of my mistake. I was ready to leave when he asked, "Can we pray?"

The church was empty, quiet, calm. Patrick walked up the side aisle ahead of me, pausing at a pew to genuflect before sitting, then kneeling. I sat in a separate place, wanting to be alone with my thoughts.

A flood of feelings swept over me. I felt a mixture of sadness and joy, of questionings and acceptance. I have learned so much and know that there is more I must learn. I know that I will need peace to accept what lies ahead. I prayed that Pat be happy, that as the months drain him he can look to me for strength. I prayed to be given that strength so that I could then give it to him. I prayed that as his mind fades even more, he not lose his thoughts of God or his spiritual faith. Above all I prayed that he have no fear.

The stillness was comforting. After a few minutes I quietly rose and walked to where Pat was. I sat by him as he continued praying. When he finished, he turned to me and held out his hand. I took it and knelt beside him. And then so that Patrick could hear, I began to quietly say a prayer out loud. It was a prayer to thank Him for the years we have had together, for the lessons we have learned, for the love we have shared. For several moments we sat in the silence. And then, ever so gently, he leaned over and kissed me.

The Hillside

In a moment of pure indulgence, I bought an ice cream cake, small enough to ease my conscience, big enough to satisfy a craving. As I placed it on the kitchen counter, I knew in an instant what I was going to do. I glanced at my watch. I then made some sandwiches and coleslaw, threw in a banana, and grabbed two paper plates.

I knew where I would go. With Pat settled in the car, I began to drive. Not quite sure of which road to take, I drove until I came to a fork that looked familiar. I followed its path and soon realized that this would, indeed, take us to the secluded, nearly forgotten place.

The large oak stood on a hillside overlooking lower meadows that faded into the bluish haze of distant trees. Pat seemed pleased. As I helped him out of the car he paused, smelling the fresh air. He looked around. He smiled.

It had been a Friday afternoon long ago when Pat had first brought me to this place. That afternoon I arrived home tired from a long week of teaching. Pat met me at the door, a bag in one hand, a bottle of wine in the other. He invited me to his car. Once inside he began to drive, responding to my inquiries with a grin but saying nothing. We had come to this spot. Climbing the hill, Pat spread a blanket on the ground while I reached in for the sandwiches he had prepared. He then produced two tall glasses, which he handed to me while he opened the bottle. The pouring wine responded with a quiet gurgling sound, momentarily breaking the stillness of this setting. We drank in silence, imbibing the fresh air, the peace, the solitude. Pat's gaze was distant, fixed on some inner thought that reflected in his expression the contentment we both felt. For the longest while we did not speak. Then quietly he turned to me. Smiling, he poured some more wine and added, "It's really pretty simple, isn't it?"

And now, so many years later, I nodded yes.

Last Month

The last couple of months have been devastating. I always thought Alzheimer's would be a slow, steady process that would quietly rob him of consciousness and memory. I relied on the fact that it would do its damage at a measured pace, giving us time to adjust and to accept. But this is too fast. It seems to set its own course, to take unexpected leaps that defy measurement. It is anything but gentle. Just last month Pat was able to get himself a glass of water and to feed himself. Today he looks at his plate of food and says he wants to eat, but makes no effort to pick up his fork. Instead he looks at his food and then at me and says, "How?" I am astounded. Just last month he could take care of his basic needs in the bathroom. Now he yells out in confusion for help. He now holds a toothbrush in his hand and seems helpless to use it. Weeks ago he would ask me to change channels on TV because he was bored with a program. Now he stares at whatever is on the screen, not really watching. Last month he took his medicine with ease. Now he struggles to swallow a single pill. One by one his abilities are being taken away, and I am powerless to do anything but watch.

Just last month …

Reality

When Dad was diagnosed with Alzheimer's, Pat decided it was time for us to look into getting long-term health care insurance. I, in my youthful denial of reality, insisted that that sort of thing would never happen to us and I really didn't want to talk about it. He calmly told me that I must face the fact that being eighteen years younger, I could financially lose everything in an effort to care for him if such a thing were to happen. He insisted on purchasing the policy.

I am getting used to the battles and daily struggles of Alzheimer's. I am fully aware of and accept the demands it places on me. What I am not prepared to face is another type of battle—the insurance company. I have held off as long as I can. But as Patrick is losing ground, I know it is time to put the long-term health care into action in order for me to receive assistance in helping him live at home.

Today the insurance company sent a health evaluator to assess Pat's condition and to set down a Plan of Care. Her test mimicked in some respects the test for Alzheimer's that his neurologist had administered. Patrick could not recall the name of the town we live in, the year, or what season it was. He had deteriorated to the point where he could no longer identify a watch when she held it up or say the word "pencil" to identify what she placed in his hand. She asked him to write something, and he produced a scribble that imitated writing only in the motion of his pen. She asked him to take off his sweater and to then put it back on. He struggled to take it off and then put it on backwards, with the three buttons now in back. He had an incontinence problem while she was here. He could barely speak, and he constantly looked to me for reassurance.

And yet her assessment is that he seems to be doing fine, that I am doing a great job, and, by the way, that he is advanced and should no longer be left alone. With a smile she said that the company would be happy to give a couple of hours a week in assistance.

I was stunned. I have reached the limit of my strength, I am surviving on less than four or five hours of sleep each night, and she thinks I am doing great. Patrick needs help. I need help. And yet it is evident that her goal is to save the company money while complying with the letter of the law and contract. Patrick is incontinent, confused, and needs to be bathed, dressed, and cared for. He wanders at night. And she feels a few hours per week will do it.

Battle

When I pleaded with the health care evaluator that I needed more hours per week, she said that her job was to assess him, and that if I felt I needed more hours I would have to appeal to the company. I told her that I was hesitant to sign my name if this were an agreement to the amount of care he would receive. She smiled and assured me that this was merely her assessment and that she had nothing to do with giving me more hours. That I had to sign to confirm the fact that she had made the health assessment. I would then have to phone the company, but rest assured that there was a way to gain more hours, and I could accomplish that by phoning the company. I got on the phone. When I explained the situation to the insurance company representative, she very politely asked, "But Mrs. Garzione, if you weren't satisfied, why did you sign?"

There it was. I was caught in the middle of a battle that was being fought with words and smiles. In every sense of the word Patrick needed help. I stressed to the company representative that I needed more hours. I described how I couldn't leave him alone for any amount of time and that despite the fact that the pharmacy and drugstore are within five minutes of the house, taking him with me was a major event. (I had already gotten a speeding ticket for trying to race home to him.) To accomplish my goal of caring for him at home, I would have to have some safeguards in place. Since I can't predict what days I will need more help or which days I will be sick, I've got to know that I will have hours available every day if I need them. I may not use them, but I've got to know the help is there. She very politely said she would get back to me.

I was angry. I said nothing. I then immediately called his neurologist, Dr. Jaeger, and Dr. Valow, his family doctor, to see if they could help. They both were extremely comforting in telling me that Patrick, indeed, needs constant care, and they would do everything to help.

And then on a late afternoon, I received a call that Patrick would receive the maximum number of hours offered under his long-term health plan. I would like to think that the insurance company made a gesture of compassion and understanding. But if, as I suspect, it resulted from the efforts of Dr. Valow and Dr. Jaeger, I will be eternally grateful to them.

Free

I was floating. I let the coolness of the water drift over me as I lay on my back and watched the ceiling slowly move in accordance to my backward strokes. It was wonderful. For one half-hour the water was mine. The time was mine. I shook my head free of water and treaded in place, smelling the distinct mixture of humidity and chlorine. Then I turned to do a lap of the pool—a freestyle of crawl, butterfly, and sidestroke. I smiled. Back home Pat was with the healthcare giver.

All needs met. All comforts given.

Solutions

On a day-to-day basis I find that I am challenged to find solutions to problems encountered.

I watched as Pat went from tying shoelaces to tying them wrong, to not knowing what to do. At first I tried to reteach him, and each time it seemed he understood. But invariably the next time he was again helpless to tie his shoes. I slowly came to the realization that once forgotten, always forgotten. Relearning a task is impossible. Rather than continually focusing on the problem, I purchased slip-on, rubber sole moccasins that I can tighten with a draw cord as needed.

I've noticed that patterns seem to perplex him. Sometimes, late at night, he hesitates when stepping from the floor onto a patterned area rug. It's as if he needs to test the stability, the firmness, before crossing over its edge. Likewise, at the dinner table he keeps tapping his plate with his fork: first the food, then the apples on the ceramic pattern. I realize he is trying to distinguish between what is real, what is edible, and what is not. I reason this has to be a problem in perception. He is struggling with boundaries—where one thing begins and another ends. So I opt for neutral-colored rugs to blend rather than stand out and use plain white plates at the table.

But moments of anxiety are hardest for Patrick. He struggles to control himself and often cannot. When he's interested in conversation or the television, this problem is minimal. However, early on I vowed to not give in to the temptation of using the television as an all-day entertainment tool. Instead, I search for activities. I have found that I can use household chores as a way of involving and holding his attention. Where once beds were made, dishes washed, things straightened well before noon in our home, now things are in ordained disarray. Throughout the day I watch for signs of anxiety or obsessive behavior. At these moments I invite him to help me. He eagerly participates and seems content to be a part of normal activities. I take great pleasure in watching him dry dishes and hold up crystal glasses to the light and smile as he admires their sparkle. I win no prize for housekeeping— beds sometimes aren't made until four o'clock. It doesn't matter.

Moccasins, white plates, peaceful disorder.

Perception

We had been watching a western on TV. I was seated in a comfy chair close to the television, glancing up now and then from the magazine I was leafing through. Pat was seated on the sofa. Suddenly he shouted, "Marilynn...over there! Go!" I looked at him. He was pointing to the chair across the room. Puzzled, I looked around. I saw no reason for the outburst, yet he was clearly agitated and kept insisting. Not until I physically moved to the other chair did he settle back to watch the gunfight on TV. And then I realized. He had seen the sheriff prepare to draw his gun. He had wanted me out of the line of fire.

What we see as two distinct realities, he perceives as one. Unable to distinguish between reality and fantasy, he has incorporated them both into a world held together with imperfect logic and reasoning. I have often thought that the results of this merger could be upsetting. The violence as portrayed on TV must at times be confusing and alarming. When Patrick sees something bad happening on TV—especially a man verbally or physically hurting a woman—he cannot control himself. Protective instincts surface. If I don't catch it in time, he will actually approach the television, striking the screen in an effort to go after the guy. Yet he openly invites positivism to his world: laughing children, slapstick comedy—all are welcomed into the room with him.

Last night I was writing a letter while he was watching TV. He turned to me. "Do we have enough?" I looked at the screen. A commercial was portraying a family arriving at the front door for Thanksgiving dinner while the grandmother was busy setting places at the table.

I smiled. "Not to worry. We have plenty."

Display

He is happy. I look at him and realize that my prayer has been answered. He enjoys life. There was a time when I thought that if you were disabled, if you had less of what you were, then you would enjoy life to that same diminished degree. That is not so. He would not have chosen this life, yet he seems content in it. He trusts that I will be here. And with the trust is the assurance that he will enjoy life with me. He had been so afraid of this. He had feared, as I had, that this disease would rob us of all happiness and well-being. Yet it seems that now, without fear and unaware of loss, his world is happy.

He wakes in the morning and reacts to my smile. He does not assess whether his life is filled with profound awareness. He seems content with the simple awareness of his surroundings. In many ways it is as if he is discovering things for the first time. He stops to point out clouds, fascinated as the sun disappears briefly behind them. He watches the birdfeeder and taps me to hush as he spots a bird fluttering on a perch. I take joy in his innocence.

The evening of the Fourth of July. I was standing by the large windows of our sunroom, watching as the trees in our backyard slowly became black silhouettes against the sky. Way up over the trees I could see a distant display of fireworks. I smiled as I looked to Pat to invite him over to see. He joined me. The sparkle of fireworks lit the southern sky. "Look, Pat! Look at the lights! Aren't they pretty?" and I pointed to the distant fireworks. "Yes, pretty," he said. But he wasn't looking up. I followed his gaze and discovered that his Fourth of July had provided him with another display of equal beauty. I turned from the explosion of lights.

Instead, we stood together and watched the gentle, quiet, flickering of fireflies as they blinked on and off in the tall grass.

The Bond

He was standing there touching the picture. For the longest while he stared at it, smiling. His hand moved gently back and forth over the glass and frame as he remained looking. It was a picture of my father. He turned to me and quietly said, "… my friend." I asked him who his friend was, and he tried, but nothing came.

And I knew. No matter how many words have been taken away, no matter how much expression was gone, the love was still there. Nothing had to be heard on the outside to confirm what was being expressed so clearly inside.

Anticipation

It had gone unopened for years. I forget which Christmas it was—probably in the first couple years of our marriage, when we had no money and struggled to buy even the most modest of gifts. I remember picking out the sweater, thinking that this purchase was way beyond our means but was something I desperately wanted for him. I had carefully wrapped it with a huge silk ribbon and bow and then proudly placed it under the tree. On Christmas Eve, with glasses of wine in hand, we settled into opening our gifts. First, there were our stockings, which we had filled with goofy nothings that were meant to bring laughter and smiles. Then I handed him the "scroll"—an annual poem I wrote for him that contained memories of the year's events, a humorous recounting of all the crazy things that had happened to us throughout the year. He always roared with laughter, reading the lines out loud and chuckling at the fact that my recollection of events was always slanted in my favor.

He was still laughing as he finally put his drink down and reached for the gift. Its ribbon spoke with anticipation of the offering inside. Then he paused and unexpectedly said, "Hon, we've already had great gifts—your poem, the goofy things in our stockings. The feeling is just perfect right now. Nothing could top this. Would you mind terribly if we held off on this one? Is it something that can keep until next year?"

I do not know why he did this, but I smiled. And so it was that each year I put that gift under the tree, and sure enough, each year Pat would hold it and smile, telling me that maybe he'd open it on Christmas morning. But he never did. Each year I perked up the bow and carefully placed it under the tree. Over the years it became a symbol of always having one more gift to open, yet opting to not open it.

Last Christmas was different. His eyes carefully took in all the presents, and when he spotted the beautiful ribbon, he reached for "our" gift. Sadly, the gift of anticipation had come to an end. But, strangely, I felt anything but sad. He had finally opened it. He held up the sweater whose color and style had long ago been forgotten. Over the years I may have lost track of what that sweater looked like, but not the memories. And for a few moments I was young again. Patrick was young again. We were sharing our first Christmas together, our future lay before us, and I had chosen the perfect gift.

Not Quite PC

We were watching TV, and I could see that he was agitated. He was grabbing at his forearm and pulling. "Honey, what are you doing?" I asked, trying to keep my voice low in order to calm him. "This stuff," he said as he kept pulling, "...what is it? It's all over. I've got to get it off ..." He continued in a vain effort to rid himself of what he thought was not right. For a second I had no idea what he meant. He was pulling harder. Then I reached over and stopped his hand. "No, Honey...that's your hair. It's all right. It's part of you. Let it alone, okay?" But it didn't seem to satisfy him. He kept pulling. "Honey, really. You're supposed to have that. You're Italian. You have it all over your arms. That's the way it's supposed to be ..." Even as I said it, I realized how politically incorrect that was, but at the moment I opted for results. He stopped. He looked and then, reaching over, ran his hand up and down my arm. "But you don't have any ..."

And lest this develop into a discussion of anatomical differences, I heard myself saying, "That's because I'm not Italian."

A Ham, I Am

It had been an easy literary choice. For years, every Christmas we both loved watching the *Grinch* as he dressed his poor helpless, yet faithful dog in antlers and descended down the mountain. Pat would chuckle the moment that deep voice began to sing ♫ *You're a mean one, Mr. Grinch...*♫ Invariably, he would then throw in his own comical lyrics to add to the description of this Yuletide ogre.

It had been years since we had shared books of mystery, biography, and adventure. Now in advanced stages, Pat eagerly seemed to respond to the light, playful style of Dr. Seuss. So in addition to reading his books, I began searching for other poets, other authors who would produce the same effect. My efforts were well rewarded, for with each new literary offering I was guaranteed his full attention:

> *Do you know that silly goat,*
> *Who tried to get into a boat?*
> *He didn't even have an oar,*
> *To row the boat to the shore,*
> *So he simply fell into the moat...*
> *Silly, willy, billy goat!*

Pat chuckled. He was enjoying the rhythm, the words, the silliness. As I started the next verse, he reached over to stop me. He smiled. From somewhere deep inside, his creative spirit had been touched. He playfully added, "Does the goat have a coat?" I burst out laughing. And then, seeing my reaction he, too, broke into a laugh that sealed the delight of this moment.

I sat back, giving a silent thank you to this children book author who, unknowingly had reached a wider audience than he had probably intended.

The Other Side

"You have no idea, Marilynn, what I'm going through right now. He's horrible. I fix dinner for him and he throws it at me. He sits in his room and curses me. I can't take his screaming. He's wearing me down. Others may be able to do this, but I can't."

Denise is a teaching colleague whose husband has Alzheimer's. By nature she is sweet, dignified. Her gentleness hides the anguish she is going through. As I listened, I wanted to tell my friend that everything would be all right. But I couldn't. I knew.

There is another side of Alzheimer's. It is a dark side, a painful side that few want to discuss but which many have to face. At any given moment, anger can burst to the surface in uncontrolled waves of hostility that over time can exhaust and abuse those trying to provide care.

Pat's asthma had been flaring up. I was giving him a treatment on the nebulizer, a machine designed to help him breathe easier. As he held the apparatus in his mouth I noticed he was breathing in too shallow, too fast. "Honey, try to breathe in with long, slow breaths, okay?"

And then it happened. He grabbed the inhaler, mouthpiece, and tubes, and in uncontrolled anger hurled them across the table, pushing himself to his feet. "You told me to do it like this!" His rage was extreme. As he stood up, he pushed me into the wall. He was out of control. "Honey, calm down," I kept repeating as I tried to get him to settle down, to no avail. Only after I followed him around the house, continually talking and reassuring him, did he begin to calm down.

I know that at any time uncontrolled anger can work its way to the surface. Things I say, gestures I make, can trigger behavior I am not trained to handle. And in those moments, I find myself almost detaching from the scene. It's as if I'm observing it from afar so that I don't have to feel it personally. It is only after he calms down that I let myself review in my mind what happened. Sometimes it helps. At other times I'm right back where I started, puzzled by his behavior and helpless to prevent it.

I was relieved when I heard that Denise's husband was put in a nursing home. The effect on her was immediate. She seemed rescued, relaxed, and able to visit him without remorse or feelings of guilt.

Home care is not for everyone. I realize that even with Pat's easy-going temperament, this side can easily surface. It is a part of the disease that I will have to learn to deal with.

Escape

In a moment of extreme anxiety and frustration, Patrick bolted for the front door.

As the need for personal care increases, so do the restrictions that limit his choices and freedom. The more he must submit to daily requests and limitations placed on him, the more he feels confined, frustrated. And when it becomes too much, he simply cannot control himself. He wants only to escape.

In an effort to prevent him from going outside in the dead of winter, I blocked the passageway, trying to persuade him to follow me back into the room. He wanted nothing to do with this house, with me or with anything that restricted him. In anger, he forcibly pushed me aside and somehow managed to undo the bolt lock. As he pulled open the door, a blast of cold air rushed in. I had little time to respond. I grabbed his coat without reaching for my own. Once outside, I caught up to him and calmly but firmly pleaded with him to come back. He kept walking in a futile attempt to distance himself from me. I draped the coat around him and resigned myself to simply walking with him. Slowly, painfully, he kept repeating, "… going home … Mom … Dad …" I shivered in the cold. *How far would he walk? Could I convince him to return? What should I do?* He stared straight ahead, neither acknowledging my presence nor responding to me.

Finally, after two blocks, he slowly came to a stop. He looked at me. He shrugged. "What do you want me to do?" was all he said. He had given up.

His pain is real. He cannot escape his frustration any more than I can escape the fact that he will never understand. I cannot convince him that I am trying to help, not control him.

Sometimes at night I listen. In a relaxed state Patrick talks in his sleep, murmuring phrases that contain no anger, no frustration. Unconscious and freed from demands made on him in the day, he is finally able to find relief. And sometimes, to my joy, he laughs and chuckles in his sleep. In his dream-state, it seems, the pain is gone. He is free.

It is reality that imprisons him.

Reflection

For every time I feel inadequate to his needs, for every time I know I haven't met the expectations I set for myself, there are other times when I know with certainty that what I am doing is right. Maybe for the moment it isn't enough, but somehow I take faith that, in the long run, adequate measure will be given. Patience. There are moments when it is evident that I have no reserve. And if in those times I do not have the necessary patience, there are other times when I know I'm giving the best that I can. It may not be what he needs at the moment; it may be a reflection of all the misgivings that I have, but it is the best I can give.

In all of this there will be times when I sit back and reflect. I did not choose to take this on. Any imperfections will have to be dealt with. I am human. Mistakes will be made.

Nocturne

When I retired, we sold the condo and moved upstate to a small house we have owned for years. It is located in a small community that unfortunately is growing fast, but that still has qualities of rural living, complete with small town charm and glimpses of wildlife. After a lot of consideration, I made the decision to build on to the house, creating a sunroom with one wall completely covered with windows. The expense was prohibitive, but the result was rewarding. As mobility is lost, Patrick can look out to see a world alive and beautiful. He never fails to look up, to call me into the room, to point out the sun, the birds.

I never realized how much we had missed when we had only a kitchen window to peer out into the backyard. Now we can see what was there for years but had gone unnoticed. Our next door neighbor has an apple tree with branches that are laden with fruit in the summer. I had never noticed the animals that come in the darkness to feast on fallen apples. Squirrels, chipmunks, and even a fat badger sit on their haunches eating the free handout.

And there was more. Even though my neighbor had told me, I did not believe it until I saw for myself. One evening, late, I was walking through the sunroom. As I turned on the light I saw a flash of movement in the backyard. I knew what it was but had to wait until the next night to verify my discovery. The next evening I waited, then called Pat in, and, in the darkness, guided him to the window.

And there they were: four deer, eating the apples, quietly muzzling the ground before lifting their heads erect to keep watch as they munched on the fruit. "Aren't they beautiful?" I whispered. I could see Pat's fascination was complete. He was mesmerized. "They're big!" he said in wonder. We watched. "Look, Hon, a baby!" He searched. "Where...?" I whispered, "Over there! Look!" The little one was moving among the larger animals and then scurried over to its mother. They were graceful, quiet, magnificent. And in the darkness we watched, not daring to move lest we interrupt the scene.

For a long while we said nothing, watching as these graceful creatures ate their nocturnal feast.

And then, in the quietest of voices, so that I could barely hear, Pat whispered, "Can we keep them?"

Rain

He had been restless for two days. Quiet talking, reading, mild distraction—nothing seemed to help. At one point I had tried to walk with him outside, hoping the bright sun would relax him. No matter what I tried, he responded with anxiety. I have learned that sometimes you just have to ride it out.

This morning was dreary and rainy. He sat with his cup of coffee in the sunroom while I played the piano in an effort to calm him. Despite a selection of his favorite songs, he seemed inattentive, distracted. After a few minutes he looked at me. He placed his hand next to him and then started patting the sofa, all the while looking to me for a response. I stopped playing.

Pat waited until I sat by him, then he tucked the blanket in around me so that we were sharing its warmth. He stretched his arm around me. I moved in close to him, thankful that in his restlessness he had reached out for me. The sound of the rain was steady, soothing. I looked around the sunroom. The wall of windows extended upward in an arch so that as the rain poured down on the glass it gave the effect of sitting under a waterfall. My thoughts drifted back …

Once as a little girl I sat on our front steps watching as a young couple walked by hand in hand. It had begun to rain, and as they hurried toward shelter, he held the edge of his jacket over her head so she wouldn't get wet. The image stayed in my mind. And my future— what would it bring? Even as a child I believed in God. I remember asking Him, "Will there be someone? Will you find me someone who will love me?" A little girl's questions, a little girl's faith.

I felt Pat's arm around me. I never dreamed anyone would love me this much. I never anticipated that all of this would be a part of our life. It was true that as a little girl I didn't think about discomfort, pain, or sickness. Now as a grown woman I understand more. There is a comfort—a kind of protection—that shields us from the future, not revealing the gifts or lessons that await us.

We sat watching the rain. The morning was no longer dreary. The rain had brought him peace.

Health Care

I came home to find them laughing. Patrick was peeking at her from around the corner, with a teasing grin on his face. Sherri was standing in the middle of the room doubled over in laughter. It didn't matter that I came onto the scene without knowing how it started. I stood there enjoying the moment and the obvious fun they were having.

I like Sherri. From the start she has been professional and caring, carefully meeting Pat's personal needs while keeping him company when I'm not there. Over the weeks and months, they have developed a comfortable, if not sweet, relationship. Sherri has become open and responsive to his playful nature. Patrick, in turn, has discovered a new audience. They seem to genuinely enjoy each others' company.

Later in the kitchen, she confided to me, "You know, Marilynn, when I started with Pat months ago I was going through a few things in my personal life. Pat is teaching me to laugh again … to really laugh."

I smiled. In the past it was Patrick who had given me the gift of laughter. Now, even unaware and with losses, he is still giving to others.

Addiction

When I opened the note, I smiled. Its sentiment touched me as I read the lines. I absorbed their meaning, slowly closed the card, and then tucked it away. I would read it again.

In early years I think I was torn between always wanting to please others while trying desperately to accept myself. I pondered endlessly about why I couldn't find ways to help all with simple strength of character. Pat never seemed to have that struggle. I remember once, long ago, reading a classroom evaluation I had received. It was a positive review, noting my strengths in the classroom, my effectiveness as a teacher, my positive influence on my students. I turned to Pat, "Yes, but why couldn't I reach that student I was telling you about? I failed with him. He hates me. I did everything wrong." Pat smiled. He always had a way of putting things into perspective. "Marilynn, you won't let go, will you! That one student, that one thing you didn't do … Why should that have more weight and power than what you are able to do? You have a glowing report here, and yet you're ignoring that to search out some negative." Later, when I couldn't help myself and again expressed my shortcomings, he stopped me. "Hon, listen. Devote as much time as you want to the negative. Do that. But don't stop there. Spend at least that same amount of time on the positive. You need a little counterbalance here."

He was right. The thing is, he lived by that. Pat could, and would, get angry or sad. He was not immune to the negative, but it never seemed to last or dominate his actions. He instinctively headed for the positive.

For Pat it was natural. For me, it is not. It is an acquired taste, and I have learned to embrace its effect. I have learned, too, that the positive is addictive. Once you get a taste of it, once you feel its strength, you can't help but want more. I've been sad. I've been happy. I prefer happy.

So now I keep a little stockpile of reminders—notes from friends and acquaintances that express encouragement, gratitude for something done, or simply a positive observation. And when I find myself slipping, surrounded by the negative, I reach for equal time.

Compassion

Years ago I was getting ready for a girls' night out. As I was about to leave I heard a crash followed by a series of expletives and discovered that Pat, barefoot, had tripped over some boxes I had left at the foot of the stairs. He was in agony, grabbing his foot as he grimaced and cursed from the mounting pain. In those years my immediate reaction to any emergency situation was panic and an inevitable flood of tears. Rather than wait for my assistance, Pat started hopping over to a chair, clinging to the edge of the table for balance. I gained enough composure to help him, all the while apologizing for my neglect at having caused the situation. When I begged that we go for an x-ray, Patrick shook his head, saying he would wait a little while to see if it got better. He insisted that there was no reason to stay. I should leave and have fun with the girls. I refused, saying that I wouldn't leave until we made sure his foot was all right. He paused and said, "Hand me that blanket. Not to worry, if it gets worse I can always drive to the hospital. Go to your party. I'll be fine." Again I stubbornly refused, trying in some small way to make up for my carelessness and lack of foresight with undying compassion.

After about twenty minutes, he turned to me and smiled. "Hey… I think it's better. Here, take a look." He pulled back the covers and lifted his foot. He then vigorously wiggled his toes and said, "See? It's fine. I'll be okay. Go have fun." Finally convinced, I left. It was only when I returned home and saw him with a cane and a tightly bandaged cast that I realized. He had shown me his other foot.

His response to pain is now different. He cannot disguise or channel his discomfort. He cannot distinguish degrees of pain. It is simply a clear signal of distress that must be addressed. And I, without panic or tears, have learned to put aside compassion and quietly assess the need.

Spring

The announcement appeared in the paper: a small art exhibit was in the nearby town, open to the public. Up to now I had always used free time to go grocery shopping, work on class preparations, or catch up on unfinished tasks. This would be the first time I sought out entertainment.

The building was located on the site of the town's tree-lined park. It was a perfect morning. In no hurry to enter, I started to walk around the duck pond. My thoughts drifted back to years ago. The ducks ...

Pat, do you remember how we used to feed the ducks? You used to watch me in silence as I reached into the bag of stale bread to take out slices. I always carefully broke them into little pieces and then gently threw my offering to the ducks eagerly awaiting the handout. You, on the other hand, would smile and simply hold out your hand. And when I handed you a slice, you would hurl the whole piece like a Frisbee beyond the ducks. You would always grin as you watched them scramble and fight for that single piece. Even with my protests of cruelty and lack of fair play, you continued hurling whole pieces of bread, laughing as the ducks continued their wild tug of war—a frenzy of feathers, water, and loud quacks.

I entered the small exhibit of modern art. One picture caught my attention. I leaned in closer to observe the brushstrokes and dabs of color. Modern art ...

Remember how much fun we had whenever we played our silly game of analyzing modern art? My mind imagined the scene; Pat was standing beside me, studying the painting: "*What do you think, Marilynn? Would you say the artist was expressing an apparent conflict of form and color in order to contribute or distract from the obvious isolation brought on by the secondary theme of emotional deprivation?*" *Pat wore a look of feigned sophistication on his face, all the while inviting me to join him in this invented game of artistic analysis. We stood there playing with words until I finally burst out laughing.* He quickly added, "*Ah, he probably just didn't give a ---!*"

As I stepped out into the crisp April morning, I took a deep breath. Spring was coming. Pat would have loved this air, the walk around the pond, the art exhibit. I smiled as I walked to the car.

The Piano

I was sad. It had started as a vague feeling of listlessness and had now taken on a stronger tone. Rather than give in to it, I sat down at the piano and let the music express what words couldn't. The piano has always done that for me. It felt good. After awhile I looked up. Pat was standing there, smiling as he watched me play. He didn't say a word.

So long ago…

It was the last month before high school graduation. I was young and apprehensive about the future. I knew within a few weeks my life would change. I would graduate and leave the island of Puerto Rico to attend college in the States. I would be leaving my family. I would also be leaving the company of Father Pat. I thought about it. In the last couple of years, he had affected my life in a way no one else had. He was just so different from anyone I had met. I had been caught unaware by his humor, his not-so-sanitized vocabulary, his love of life. But most of all I had been affected by his belief in God. He had challenged me to look beyond the surface—beyond language and stereotypes—to find a deeper meaning of belief and conviction.

That night I was restless and couldn't sleep. I got up and quietly left our darkened housing quarters to walk to the base chapel a few blocks away. Dad's office was next to the chapel, and I knew the annex building would be open. There was a piano in this side building where services were sometimes held, and I knew even at this late hour I would be able to be alone and play.

The keyboard felt comfortable, and I found it soothing to express myself in music. I can't recall how long I had been playing, but I became more aware of my surroundings when I saw a light turn on in a distant office room. I continued playing but listened carefully when I heard footsteps approaching. I looked up. It was Father Pat. He stood in the doorway as I continued playing. He smiled then quietly walked over to me. "Nice," he said, and then gently added, "It's late, Marilynn . You shouldn't be here alone. Come on … I'll walk you home." The military base was safe, well guarded, but his words were comforting.

I remember walking out into the warm air, heavy with the smell of honeysuckle. He didn't know my growing, confused feelings for him. He probably never would. But for a few minutes on a warm night in Puerto Rico, we walked together.

The Name

In the early morning hours I lay in bed with Pat, watching him sleep. I smiled. Today was a special day. As I stirred, he opened his eyes. After a few seconds he focused on me. He reached toward me and I turned, letting his arms envelop me.

"Happy anniversary, Honey." I smiled. "Today is our anniversary." He asked, "It is?" and I knew he had no idea what the word meant nor its significance. "Yes," I said gently, "we were married on this day a long time ago. This is the day I became your wife." He paused for a few seconds then said, "Wife ... you ... that's very good." He smiled and then touched my face. "You're my girl."

"Yes, Pat."

He seemed pleased. He pushed his pillow aside and looked at me. He gently smiled. He struggled for words. "You, me, here ... you live ... you are here?"

A thousand thoughts flashed through my mind. *Has he forgotten? Have I lost him?* But in that instant I knew. He was asking for reassurance. "Yes, I will always be with you, Honey." Once again he smiled. He ran his hand up and down my arm then stroked my hair.

And without knowing why, I whispered, "Hon ... do you know my name?" He looked at me with such warmth and innocence, then he paused. There was silence. And then, slowly, with an honesty that bore witness to great loss, he whispered, "No ..."

My voice failed me. The reality of this moment stunned me. Struggling to hold in emotions, I whispered, "That's okay, Honey. Marilynn ... my name is Marilynn."

"Marilynn," he slowly repeated as he again touched my face and smiled. "Of course ... Marilynn."

I had often wondered when this moment would come, and now it had. For a second I was totally absorbed in loss. Then, as I looked into his face, I realized that despite all this, everything had not yet been taken away. He is still here. He still cares for me; he still loves and desires my presence. My name may be lost, but he knows *me* ... only the name is missing.

I can accept this. I can accept this, knowing that it is preparing me for the time when he no longer remembers me. That will come, but not now.

I nestled closer to him, comforted by his warmth.

Choice

Alzheimer's is a horrible disease. It is not built solely of beautiful memories or precious moments. The truth is that its harsh reality sometimes forces you to push aside the positive in order to face the full impact of its negative power. I can't recall when I first knew that this disease was stronger than my determination to match, step by step, its progress. Intellectually I knew, of course, that it would win, but it has taken repeated revelations for me to realize that I am limited, that I have limited endurance.

In an effort to manage the problem of incontinence, I stocked up on Depends and disposable bed pads. Yet sometimes efforts to get him to the bathroom or to aide him in sitting are met with resistance. When cleaning up a messy accident for the second or sometimes third time in one day, I have come to realize that effort and preparation sometimes have little impact on the situation. When food is rejected, when medications are spit out, when obsessive behavior is dominating the day, I am forced to see that even my best efforts to provide adequate care are simply not enough. And sometimes when anxiety destroys all his self-control and I am faced with verbal or even physical violence, my mind has reached for relief. It is at the point of pure exhaustion and helplessness that I have wondered how I can possibly continue to meet his needs.

I, like Patrick, am not immune to the far-reaching effects of Alzheimer's. I cannot escape its reality. But I know that I have choices. If I can choose to accept its pain, I can also choose to find relief from it. I can focus on those moments that will edify rather than destroy, that will nourish and sustain. I can choose to rely on what experience has taught me—that by looking past the negative I can find strength in the positive. It is my way of not giving in. It is my way of seeking a renewed spirit so that I can help Patrick cling to a life that still longs to be expressed.

Blind

Caring for someone with Alzheimer's is not in itself an impossible task. It is just so *constant*. When measured by one day, it is definable, do-able. When measured against the relentless progression of days, nights, weeks, and months, the absence of relief leaves only the awareness that the same need for care awaits you tomorrow, and the next day, and the next.

As soon as my healthcare giver arrived, I got into the car. I was tired. The preceding days had exhausted me physically and emotionally, until I felt I had nothing left inside to give. I needed to go to the one place that had become a refuge of comfort and renewal.

I climbed the hill again. It was raining, but I did nothing to stop the wetness from pouring over me. It felt cool and good. When I reached the tree where we had sat drinking wine, I paused.

Pat, you had said it was all so simple. But how can it be simple when everything feels complicated—when everything in me is tired—when I have so little to give?

I looked up. It all looked different. It had been so beautiful before. Now the mist was hiding the lower fields and fusing everything into a rainy gray blanket of dreariness. I tried to make out the shape of trees at the far end of the meadow. I could see nothing.

Wait, Marilynn. Wait until this passes, and you will see again. Wait for the light, and you will again see the meadows, the trees ... the beauty. Hang on. You'll see. It will be simple again.

135

The Ride

As we were getting into our car after leaving the supermarket, Pat suddenly turned to me and held his arms out wide. His face lit up. He pointed in a general outward direction and asked, "Us ... out there?" I smiled and nodded. After a quick stop at the deli for coffee, we began to drive along winding country roads. At every crossroad, I asked him to choose the direction we would take. He reacted with enthusiasm, pointing, then chuckling, while I turned the wheel.

As his mobility is diminishing, it is becoming harder for him to take walks. But his spirit is still eager to explore, to discover. So in moments of boredom or restlessness I will often ask him, "How about it, Hon—want to take a ride?" knowing full well that it's an offer he can't refuse.

We are lucky in that we live in an area that still has country charm. At almost any turn, a new road reveals itself, along with its scattered farms and wooded areas. It doesn't matter that I sometimes choose the same route. Whether he recognizes the scenery or not, he always enjoys the drive, pointing out things along the way or simply turning to me and smiling. I find myself slowing down, allowing other cars to pass, so that he can pick up details that would otherwise be missed.

I slipped in a CD. As the first notes of *Smokey Joe's Café* filled the car, Pat started to beat his knee in rhythm, humming the melody of songs familiar to him. Before long, we were both singing at the top of our lungs, matching the lyrics or simply making them up. It was less a faithfulness to the music of Leiber and Stoller than a need for unbridled expression. It didn't matter that Pat no longer knew the words. He moved to the rock-and-roll beat and sang along with nonwords, contributing in a doo-wop sort of way.

♫ *I'm goin' to Kansas City ... Kansas City here I come!* ♫

Who's On First?

The morning had gone smoothly, and Patrick was almost dressed.

"Okay, Honey ... we better finish getting dressed so we can go."

"Where are we going?"

"We're going to see the doctor for a checkup. Here. Here's your socks."

I watched as he carefully took a sock and stretched the top before placing his foot inside. After repeating the same action with the other sock, he studied both feet. He seemed satisfied. Looking up at me, he smiled.

"Are we going for a ride?"

"Well ... we're riding to the doctor's office."

"Doctor?"

"Yes, Dr. Valow. You remember her. She's a nice doctor."

He nodded, "... he's a nice doctor."

"Yes ... well, *she* wants to see how you're doing."

"She?"

"Yes, it's Dr. Valow. She's a doctor."

He stared at me. His face became serious.

"She's a man?"

He looked at me with an incredulous expression. I hurried to set matters straight.

"No, she's a doctor."

He looked at me intently.

"He's a she?"

I smiled, "No, no, no, no ... she's a doctor. We'll be with her ... we're going to be with her, your doctor."

Patrick pondered the situation.

"Oh ... we're riding with the doctor?"

"No, we're riding *to* the doctor. Here. Here's your shoe."

He took the shoe. Holding it in his hand, he paused for several seconds before once again turning his attention to me.

"He's not coming with us?"

Some days communication is less effective than others. I waited until he finished putting his shoes on. "There. All ready. Let's get going." I helped him to his feet, and we headed for the front door. As I opened it, Pat paused. He looked outside and smiled.

With eager curiosity he asked, "A ride? Where are we going?"

The Store

I have found that Patrick's behavior in public can, at times, be unpredictable. His appearance is deceptive. He does not look sick. In fact, his energy and enthusiasm give the impression of a much younger and healthier man. When people look at him or engage him in conversation, they do not expect what sometimes awaits them.

We had gone to the little candle store located on the edge of town. In the past this was a favorite place—an old wooden structure with many nooks and crannies filled with teddy bears, lace pillows, soaps, and candles. With things to touch and pick up, it is now the perfect place for Patrick to feed his curiosity and interest. On this occasion, we spent considerable time browsing through the main part of the store. We then headed to a small corner hidden far in the back. Once there, I exchanged smiles with a lady who had also found the charm of this narrow passage tucked away from the main part of the store.

And then I heard it. A quiet one at first, but definitely audible. I nudged Pat. "Honey, we don't do that in public." A few seconds later I heard another, this time louder. "Honey, I mean it. Not here ... wait 'til you get home." It did no good. The lady was trying not to react, looking intently at a teddy bear. In silent dignity she began picking up more teddy bears. Then in the silence he trumpeted again. "Honey!" He simply responded, "... but I have to!" The sound, not to mention the atmosphere, was becoming intolerable. The poor lady had had enough. Clearly a captive in the corner, she was now trying to find an escape route, but found instead Patrick blocking the way.

With a mumbled attempt at "Excuse me," the trapped shopper finally managed to squeeze past us. Pat looked at her and, as she passed, loudly proclaimed, "She does it too!"

Trip to Bethlehem

Near our house is a tiny church situated on a hill, named Bethlehem Church. Built in 1729, it dates back to a simple era when worship was intended for the few devoted settlers of the community. I love this tiny church. When filled to capacity, fewer than a hundred people can be seated, yet its unadorned Protestant architecture and intimate setting were the very elements that drew Patrick and me to this house of worship, especially on Christmas Eve.

Tonight I brought Patrick with me to once again share in the evening candlelight service. It was a quiet gathering that offered the faithful a chance to share in simple carols and quiet music. Patrick had been restless all day, showing signs of increased anxiety, and I thought the peacefulness of this setting would soothe and quiet him. With that in mind, I entered the church and spotted an empty pew in the back. I chose an aisle seat in order to exit should that become necessary.

The lights dimmed. The service began. The tiny congregation hushed as the quiet tones of the church piano began a soft flowing introduction. In the quietness, a single voice began to sing "O Holy Night." With candles as the only illumination, the entire church seemed to flicker in accompaniment to the soft, soothing lyrics. The effect was peaceful, tranquil. I closed my eyes.

I felt a soft tapping on my shoulder. Looking up, I saw a young woman leaning toward me. She whispered, "Excuse us, would you mind moving over?" I smiled and quietly whispered back, "If you don't mind—my husband has Alzheimer's—we may have to leave. Do you mind if we sit on the aisle?" She smiled. "Of course."

With some difficulty I proceeded to assist Patrick as he unsteadily rose to his feet in order to allow the couple to squeeze past us. Despite all good intentions, the awkwardness of that attempt made me realize that the pew was too narrow for their passage. I then took his hand and quietly urged him to follow me into the aisle while the couple then slid into the pew. He begrudgingly followed. Once they were situated in the pew, I then reversed the procedure, asking Pat to now step back in to sit down.

Confused and disturbed, Patrick had had enough. In the middle of "O Holy Night"—in the midst of the silence and peacefulness of this tiny gathering—came a booming voice:

"Let's get the hell out of here!"

We did.

Relapse

In the first weeks of April, he became sick. Pat was always subject to the effects of asthma, and his condition quickly developed into pneumonia. He was treated with antibiotics and stronger inhalant medicines and rapidly improved.

But now, three weeks later, the symptoms are back. Once again I brought him to the doctors and returned home with renewed prescriptions for antibiotics, inhalants, and cough medicine. His breathing comes in wheezes—labored and shallow. And now the steroids in his inhalant medicine have made him agitated.

Early in the evening he had an asthma attack. Once the initial attack was over, I tried desperately to alleviate his discomfort. He could not sleep. I propped his back up with pillows so that he could breathe easier. I could hear that his breathing was still labored, and I questioned whether I should take him in to the doctors again. Maybe in the morning. His coughing was deep, disturbing. How I wish I had training in medicine!

I tried to soothe him, telling him to relax, to try to sleep. He could not. He tried hard to follow my instructions, visibly relaxing between bouts of heavy breathing, but in the wee hours of the morning he could take no more. He was agitated and confused. Between gasps and coughing spells he looked at me. "This ... why?"

I tried to explain that he was sick, that the medicines would help him soon, but that it would take a little time. He was inconsolable. He was trying to find reasons for his discomfort. "Why? Did I do something?" I explained again that no, he was sick, that we had gone to the doctors, that they had given him medicine that should soon help him. "They did this?" I shook my head. With an anguished expression he asked, "Why did they do that?" I could not make him understand.

Throughout the night he woke in starts as his coughing and wheezing continued. And despite my efforts, I had no comforting answer as he kept murmuring, "Why?"

Why

I lay back and thought about his question. Why Pat? Why us?

It dawns on me: Why not us? Why not Pat? We aren't so very different from other people. We aren't special. What makes our lives so different that we should never have been given this? Why should we be immune to what thousands have had to endure? We hear of so many tragedies in this world and always compare them to the stability of our own well-being. We are safe. We are not *them*.

And when we do become the unfortunate ones, it suddenly feels like we've been pushed into an unfair world that was meant to be distant from our lives.

But this *is* us now. We weren't chosen to be special or protected from disease. We are a part of it. And if Pat were able to have an understanding of *why*, if his mind could comprehend, he would still be left with the same question. With or without understanding, it would remain unanswered.

The Secret

She had been watching me work with Pat. When we were alone, she turned to me and said, "Marilynn, you have so much patience ... how do you manage it?"

I smiled. She didn't know the truth. She didn't know the secret. I know that much of what I am able to give Pat was learned through experience and effort. But not everything. I am absolutely convinced that patience isn't so much in the giving as it is in the perception. And I know very well that some of what I give isn't genuine at all. I'm not made of all genuine. Inside I'm filled with feelings of frustration that scream to be let out. Yet I know their release will serve no purpose. Release will, in fact, work against me if I give in to anxiety and convey that to him. So at times it is, quite frankly, faked patience.

It's easy to be patient when it's bright outside, when you're well rested, when there are no challenges to time and giving. But wait until nighttime. You have already completed a day, you're tired, and your guard is down. At 12:45 you get up to find him confused, refusing to go back to bed. You quiet him. Then you are up again at 1:30 to help him in the bathroom. At 2:00, you drag yourself out of bed to again try to convince him that it's time to sleep, not walk through the house. It takes several minutes to sit with him and gradually lure him back to bed. By the time you get up at 3:45, you realize that even this will not be the last time before morning. You will be up again. You are also aware that morning is fast approaching and with it a whole new day to deal with. These are the moments when it's so easy to give in to impatience. It is then that I go into my "fake mode"—patience balanced on a thin layer of ice that is being chipped away by the needs of another.

I force myself to remember a scene from *The King and I*. It is the story of Anna, a young widowed schoolteacher who arrives in Siam with her young son. Filled with anxiety and fear, mother and son prepare to leave the ship. To help her son be brave she sings a sentiment that holds a lot of truth:

> *Make believe you're brave and the trick will take you far,*
> *You may be as brave as you make believe you are...*

And so I am patient—a completely fake version of the real thing. But whether it's real or fake, it serves the same purpose. He perceives it as patience. It's what he needs at the moment. It works.

Fries

He sat across from me licking the salt from his fingers. He looked up. "I like these!" he said enthusiastically. I smiled. We had gone from salads and bean sprouts to french fries.

A part of me felt guilty. Perhaps because I never did get hooked on health food, perhaps because there would always be a part of me that preferred a milkshake to green tea, I had somehow let junk food creep back into our diet. It had been a cold evening after a late doctor's appointment. Rather than face the thought of going home to cook, I saw the familiar symbol of a famous food chain. I gave in to the urge to both satisfy my cravings and solve the dinner problem. I was surprised and pleased that he didn't object. He had always shied away from fast food. In fact, he had always been a champion of nutrition.

I remember past images of Pat in the kitchen squeezing vegetables into an electric juicer. "Here, try this …" he said, handing me a glass of freshly produced carrot/celery/red beet juice. I took a sip. He grinned as he watched me struggle to down the bitter albeit healthy drink. "Great stuff, huh?" My reaction was less than positive. He smiled, "Okay, okay. Next time I'll put in a few apples. You'll learn to like it—you'll see!" I never did.

At the least sign of a cold he was there to hand me Ester-C and a bottle of herbal echinacea goldenseal extract. An on-coming ailment would trigger a MacGyver-type dedication to concoct a healthy homemade remedy. "Come on … it's good for you." In the fridge was a bottle of aloe vera for burns, and I suspect that somewhere in our archives of magazines were old issues of *Mother Earth News*.

The Italian in him never refused a glass of wine or ethnic food. On more than one occasion I remember watching in horror as he chopped up cloves of raw garlic, covered a chunk of semolina bread with it, then drizzled olive oil, salt, pepper, and Italian parsley on top. I cringed as he bit into it, unable to watch. He would always enjoy my reaction and, pausing, would innocently proclaim with his mouth full, "Whaaat?! Garlic is good for you!" And then, knowing full well the aftereffects of this snack, he would teasingly pursue me, laughing all the while as he tried to kiss me. "Hey—I'm just trying to be affectionate!"

Sorry, Pat…some things are definitely in the past. I smiled and watched with satisfaction as he stuffed in another french fry.

Purpose

Pat once told me of a time when, as a young priest living in Taiwan, he flew on a weekend pass to Hong Kong. While there he stayed with an elderly priest he was fond of, and together they enjoyed this time of renewed friendship. Because of the effects of some over-celebrating, Pat was convinced at the last minute to stay over and take a later flight back. The plane took off without him. Five minutes into the flight, it crashed into a mountain, killing all aboard. Patrick told me that the next day he read accounts of the crash, and there, listed among the dead, was his name.

Years later, while serving on the D.E.W. Line near the Artic Circle, he was aboard a transport plane with several men as they flew to a distant site. Without warning the entire side door of the cargo hatch blew off, causing a drop in cabin pressure and a drastic loss of altitude and directional navigation. For several harrowing minutes the pilot struggled to regain control, circling the ice field in an effort to land. Pat related how, in silence, each man came to grips with the situation and prepared for the crash landing. Somehow the crippled plane was able to force land on the ice cap. Pat smiled when he said the chapel tent was filled to capacity the next Sunday.

Why had his life been spared both times? His life could so easily have ended when he was young. I never would have met him; people would never have been helped or influenced by him. The world would have never even have known of his existence. And yet I cannot think that life is a collection of random events that have no meaning. Perhaps even pain and loss are something we are incapable of understanding, but which fit into a higher order of reason and purpose.

The Sound

As I drove up to the building complex that housed the doctor's office I weighed my options. I could park in the only available space on the far side of the parking lot, or I could pull up to the curb, get Patrick into the building, and park the car while he waited in the office.

I glanced at Pat. He was tapping on the car window in time to the music of the CD. I smiled. It promised to be a quick, easy visit. I pulled up to the building and stopped in the passenger-unloading zone. Getting out of the car, I walked around to Pat's side.

There are some sounds so familiar we are able to identify them even without visual cues—the popping of a champagne bottle, the crack of a bat hitting a baseball, the shattering sound of breaking glass. As I approached his door I heard it—the totally distinct and familiar *click* that stopped me in my tracks. I didn't have to look to know what it was.

Absurdity and frustration combined to produce a laughable if not lamentable picture. There I was tugging at a locked door I knew wasn't going to open while Patrick stared at me from the other side. Far from being frightened or disturbed, he seemed curiously interested in this turn of events. I tapped the window near the lock button. Patrick tapped back. I motioned for him to push the lock. He tapped the glass. I smiled at him, shaking my head in disbelief at how I could have gotten into this mess. Patrick chose the moment to smile and wave at me.

Repetition. I kept pointing to the toggle button that controlled the lock, gesturing to Patrick in the hope that he would somehow push the upper portion to unlock the door. Every time his hand approached the toggle, I clapped and nodded, eagerly encouraging him to push it. But, alas, each time he found the button he kept pushing it down instead of up.

By this time another car had pulled up, and the woman driver asked if she could help. I certainly was open to suggestions, but the fact was clear that, with the keys still in the ignition and the car running, there were few options. I reached for my cell phone to call the police.

Then, as quickly as it had started, it was over. By accident and through no willful intention, Patrick hit the upper portion of the lock

148

button. The same sound that a few minutes earlier had been met with woeful resignation was now greeted with joyful relief. The lock popped up and I quickly opened the door. I was laughing as I helped him onto the curb.

And reacting to my laughter, Patrick smiled and stuck out his tongue.

Alone

I found him sitting in a chair, alone in the living room. There were tears in his eyes. I quietly went to him. "Is something wrong, Honey? Are you alright?" He looked at me. Slowly, quietly, he formed the words, "It's better this way." My heart sank. He leaned his head back, looking at the ceiling, and then slowly turned his head toward the window and looked out. I gently asked again, but he was unresponsive. I tried to take his hand, but he quietly withdrew it.

I will never know what he meant by those words or what he was feeling. Perhaps he had a moment of total awareness. Perhaps for brief seconds he knew the full extent, the full impact, of what his world had become. I do not know. I felt tears welling in my eyes and quickly looked away so he would not see. In the minutes that followed, I sat with him. I did not try to talk him out of it or make him respond to me. I simply wanted him to know that I was there if he wanted to reach out. Yet even with me next to him, he was alone in his pain.

After a few minutes I put on a music CD, softly so that it wouldn't interrupt, yet there for him if he chose to listen. For a long while he did not respond. And then, true to his nature, he turned toward the music. At first he sat looking straight ahead, listening quietly. Then slowly, gently, his hand took mine. Time was having an effect. As the music continued, Patrick began to listen more to the rhythms and melodies. I looked down. I smiled.

His foot was tapping in time to the music. He had come back.

The Question

We had been chatting over a cup of coffee, talking about goals, places we have always wanted to visit, things we have always wanted to do. In the course of our conversation my friend gently turned to me and asked, "Marilynn, have you given any thought to ... you know ... *after?*" In any other circumstance, I might have felt offended by the abruptness of the question, but at this moment it seemed natural, expressed with the sincerity of a friend concerned for my welfare.

The truth is, I don't know. Yes, the thought has come to my mind, but each time I have pushed it aside. Strangely, my whole life has always been guided by goals and a determination to complete projects I've begun. But this is different. To think ahead feels like a betrayal of the now, an exclusion of him. I know that the future will come, that there will be an *after*, but it's the one thing I refuse to think of. I know it will come, and I may very well be unprepared. But I will not think of or prepare for a time without him.

Unaware

We had been standing in line at the cash register at the grocery store. Patrick was eyeing the items in the cart of the lady in front of us. Spotting a gallon of chocolate ice cream in her basket, he eagerly reached over and placed it in our cart. I smiled as I reached out to Pat, who by now was headed for her potato chips. The woman watched in shock, completely at a loss for words and unsure how to react. I quietly intervened. "Alzheimer's," I said as I quickly returned the ice cream to her cart. With recovered dignity and compassion she said, "I'm so sorry. It must be awful!" I paused. Should I tell her? Should I risk shocking her again? Patrick was now cheerfully refocused and studying the Twinkies that topped the items in her basket. Then his attention was drawn to two balloons tied to her cart. For several seconds he looked at them and then at me. Smiling, he carefully untied one and, in a spontaneous gesture, offered it to me. Touched by this show of affection, I reached out. I smiled as I saw how pleased he seemed. Accepting his simple gift, I held the balloon and turned to her. Knowing that she, too, had witnessed this gentle display of affection, I said, "You know, everything you hear about Alzheimer's is true—but what they don't tell you is that there are good moments, too."

She looked at me. In quiet disbelief she said softly, "Oh?...Name me one."

Darkness

Last night the electricity went out. We had been watching TV, and in an instant we were in darkness. Pat immediately wanted to go to bed, but since it was only 9 o'clock, I knew that would only invite an up-in-the-night or early-in-the-morning awakening, when I'm at my worst. So in the dark Pat walked behind me, both hands on my shoulders as we slowly shuffled our way to the darkened sunroom. There, the dim outside light would enter.

We sat in the dark, bundled up in a blanket, and "talked." Although I couldn't understand the major part of what he was saying, Patrick seemed eager to speak. I patted his arm and added an occasional "Ahuh…" as he kept talking. I was receiving visual images from his sentence fragments but had little idea as to what he was describing. I sat back and listened.

"A big place," he began and then he paused to capture his thought. "For awhile we were here and then we were there … Little babies coming out." He paused again. "It was finished … the sun was big … happy babies …"

And then in an instant I knew. The day before, Sherri, his healthcare giver, had asked if he'd like to go with her to the next town to pick up her little girl after school. He was remembering. He was telling me of his special afternoon.

"Little boy … girl … happy babies ran …"

And I knew that in the darkness he was smiling.

Secret Santas

I woke up to a snowy world. For a moment I absorbed its beauty, and then, seeing that the snow was coming down hard, my thoughts turned to more practical matters. I glanced at Patrick. I had given him his early morning meds, and once again he was sleeping. I knew I would have a small window of time. I quickly bundled up, grabbed some gloves, pulled on some boots, and headed for the garage. After checking the snowblower for oil and gas, I pumped the primer and pushed the automatic start button. Nothing. I checked the electric cord and all connections—everything my unmechanical mind could think of. I tried the starter again. Still nothing. After several attempts with no success, I resigned myself to search for the shovel.

After an hour of heavy shoveling, it was apparent that I could go no further. The snow was gaining, and I was beginning to feel light-headed. I gave up. Mindful of the fact that soon Pat's day would begin, I headed back inside. The snow continued to fall.

The next two hours were filled with meds, hygiene, dressing, and breakfast. Then, as I was walking through the living room, I heard the sound of a motor. I looked out and spotted a man snowplowing our driveway. For a few seconds I watched, and then I grabbed my coat. As I approached, he looked out from his fur-lined parka hood and smiled. I recognized him as our neighbor from across the street. I thanked him, and as I attempted to hand him some money, he stopped me. "No way! Put that away!" I begged him to accept. He continued, "No. One of the nicest gifts I got this year was that Christmas note you left in our mailbox." For a second my mind drew a blank.

Then I remembered. This Christmas they had decorated their front yard with wonderful blinking candy canes, Santas, and shimmering lights that covered a tall pine tree. Every night as we walked into the bedroom Pat would walk over to the window. "Look!" he would say, pointing to the sparkling lights across the street. And each night before going to bed we would stand together in the dark, admiring the silent beauty of the scene. The day after Christmas I had written a note thanking them for their priceless gift of light.

He continued. "Thank you … it just made me realize how sometimes there are simple things we do that affect others without us

154

even knowing it. My wife generally takes the decorations down the day after Christmas. You can bet that from now on we're leaving them up until after New Years!"

I smiled, realizing that, unaware, we had just exchanged gifts.

Soft Comfort

He's forming a world around what is left. As his vocabulary decreases, he seems to rely on set phrases and key words. He sometimes speaks in the abstract, often repeating a phrase over and over in an effort to make me understand. There appears to be an internal logic that allows him to insist on what he is saying, even if the phrase seems totally illogical to me. And while, for the most part, I manage to pull the word fragments together, there are times when I simply admit to him that I do not understand.

When I speak he listens, trying desperately to comprehend. If I am referring to something in the room, I will point, setting a reference he can understand. But he has lost perception of space. He cannot follow my finger to see the intended object. He simply stares at whatever captures his attention.

And despite his effort to communicate, there are times when he gives up. He simply mumbles something to indicate that it is not important and then settles into silent resignation. At those times I try to encourage him to explain what he wants or needs, but often he does not.

And yet he tries. He instinctively struggles to find words to reach me. He wants to communicate. And with communication comes comfort. For me it is no longer the comfort of words.

It is the soft comfort of his voice.

The Fair

Tony's Italian Sausage and Peppers. The sign hadn't changed over the years. The stand had belonged to Pat's father and is still part of the annual summer fair. Pat used to talk of the countless summers of his youth when he would help his father run the stand, sleeping in the back at night, working the grills, handling the crowds. Years back Pat and I would ride up in August to help clean peppers and pitch in to help his brother-in-law who, after Tony, ran the stand until his retirement.

Last week we drove up to the fair. After a few minutes of wandering along the fairway to see the 4-H animals, we walked to the booth. Pete, his nephew, now runs the sausage stand, and he greeted Pat with his usual warmth and affection. As they talked, I looked around. There on the side of the booth was the picture of Pat's father. Taken sometime back in the early 50s, it showed a proud Tony standing in front of his stand, apron on, ready to greet customers. I could see Pat in him: the same build, the same stature, the same dark hair … the same smile. They say, like Pat, Tony had a playful nature; he was always laughing, always seeking to make others laugh. I smiled as I imagined him alive, robust, proud.

Today, alone, I went to the cemetery. *Anthony and Helen Garzione.* For a few minutes I remained in thought. I had never met them. I knew that because their son had been a priest, they undoubtedly would not have accepted me. They could never have approved of my being a part of his life. I understood. I ran my hand over the stone letters. I thanked them for caring for Patrick, for giving him love all those years. I wanted them to know how grateful I would always be. I wanted them to know, too, that I was caring for their son the best I could. And then, quietly, I told them that until they were together again, he would not be alone.

The Truth

Anxiety is tearing him apart. He struggles to recognize his surroundings, yet he cannot escape the pain of confusion. He doesn't know what to do, cannot express himself, and is helpless to find relief. Hostility and aggression are a natural result, as more and more is taken away from him. Three days ago in a moment of extreme agitation, he ripped the towel rack off the wall in the bathroom. At that moment I had to distance myself from him, for safety as well as to not aggravate him further. I tried repeatedly to let him know that I am here, that I will take care of him, comfort him. But the painful truth is that he can no longer take comfort in me because he no longer knows who I am.

He needs medical help. Dr. Jaeger, his neurologist, has been with him since his first diagnosis. Always attentive and sensitive to Patrick, he has sought to follow the course of this disease with medications that can delay, or at least ease, the progressive nature of Alzheimer's. I called him.

He listened as I described Patrick's agitation and aggressive behavior. Seeing that the medication he was taking was no longer effective, Dr. Jaeger changed drugs, opting for another that might calm him so that he can be cared for. When Patrick turns aggressive, when he seeks only to escape, he will not allow me to approach him, to clean him, to touch him. He lashes out in a vain attempt to gain control, to regain his world. He cannot.

Relief came in the form of new medication. The pills are designed to calm him. They will never cure, never eliminate the disease. They will simply ease somewhat the terrible tension and pain he must be feeling. Within hours I could see that the new medication was helping. For the moment the discomfort is gone. For the moment he is at peace. He is smiling again. I know this is not forever. Forever is not an option. But for now he can once again interact with life around him. He once again reaches for my hand, and I am grateful.

The raw truth is that no medication, no action—on my part or that of Dr. Jaeger—is going to do anything to prevent the relentless power of this disease. He will lose.

My promise is to gently help him lose.

Remembering

He is fading away. So much has been taken away that I find myself searching for anything that I can still hang onto. I have given him away. I have given him away to medications, to doctors, to homecare aides, to all the daily tasks I do that rob me of what was. I can't remember a time when there weren't the meds, the plastic gloves, the ointments, the lotions. It is the sterile, antiseptic smell of a home-made hospital. And now I can't even remember what he used to smell like. This morning I had to get away from all that. I longed for something, anything, that would remind me of what he still is. I went into the bathroom and closed the door. I shut out the world. I needed to search for him. I opened the medicine cabinet, and among the prescriptions, toothpaste, and mouthwash I found it. I held the bottle in my hands as I sat on the edge of the bathtub and slowly opened it. As I lifted the cap, the smell of his aftershave lotion filled my senses, and I closed my eyes.

I remembered.

Despair

I can't do this. Patrick, you once promised me that you'd always be there when I needed you ... why aren't you here now when I need you the most? I wasn't meant to be the strong one. You were. You were supposed to be my mentor, my guide, my strength. You promised for always. How can I possibly do what is right, when every day, every hour you are slipping further away and can never tell me?

This morning I feel so alone.

I Can

Strength isn't natural. It isn't something that you can assume will be there. It isn't something constant, nor is it even something you can rely on. I think it's more *will* than strength. A stubborn determination that you will not give in to any feeling that will, in turn, leave you helpless to act. I remember watching Nancy Reagan as she clung to the coffin of her husband, unable to let go. I understood. At that moment I was silently praying for her: "You can do this, you can do this," as if my prayer would somehow give her strength. I understand what Pat so often told me in the past: to not worry if you don't feel any strength inside. In those moments, look to others and use theirs. And maybe that is what friends and loved ones are for. Because in the end, it was Nancy's children who came to help her walk away.

And I have learned, too, that in searching I have found it ... that every time I have asked for strength, it has been given to me.

Hidden Gifts

I couldn't sleep. I grabbed my bathrobe and stood by the window looking out into the darkness. The stillness was comforting, and the quiet echoed what I felt inside. I released my mind ...

It has been such a long journey. So much has happened, so much has changed. I have gone through levels of awareness and gained a perspective that is now uniquely mine. I look at myself and know that as painful as this has been, this disease has changed me in ways I would never have imagined. I have finally come to understand that if you look only at the disease, you will see only the disease. If you only focus on the pain, you will feel only that pain. Yet I have seen and felt so much more. I have been given moments of laughter that have prepared me for moments of sorrow. I have been given support and encouragement that have sustained me in times of profound weakness. I have seen that there is life going on around this disease, and I have come to embrace and celebrate its right to exist. And I have been given love—a love given unaware by one who can no longer know the full value of its strength.

I wonder ... If given the opportunity to change what is, would I?

Of course. I would sell my soul, wipe away time, give up everything, every strength, every lesson learned, to take away his pain. But without the power to enact, the exercise of thought is useless. I know that it all comes down to acceptance.

And I accept.

Now

It was early morning when I tiptoed into the bedroom. Patrick was awake, eyes open in a staring gaze, looking at the ceiling. As I quietly approached the bed, his head turned slightly and he looked at me. He had a puzzled look on his face—the look I have seen so often and have come to recognize. He was lost, afraid.

I held my hand out to him and slowly sat on the bed close to him, leaning over so he didn't seem so far away. All the pain was gone, all the past seemed to fade, and what was left was this moment ... the quiet, gentle now. He looked into my eyes, searching for what he needed to know. Slowly he found the words and softly, quietly, he asked, "Am I home?" I pulled the covers up close and gently stroking his forehead I whispered, "Yes, Patrick, you are home."

And then, like a child comforted, his face became serene, and he closed his eyes.

Note to the Reader

Weeks later, following a brief hospital stay, Patrick entered into hospice care. In the early morning hours on a Sunday in March, Patrick died quietly, peacefully, at home. Marilynn was at his side.

Front Cover Photo: Taken on the morning of Patrick's death, this photo of the sunrise carries with it the promise of a new day and the joy of life renewed.

A Personal Message

Since Patrick's death, I have discovered and embraced the efforts of the Alzheimer's Association. Early in the year I was invited to go with Hudson Valley representatives to Albany to share my story with members of the New York State Legislature. I had misgivings and apprehensions—my personal experiences are sometimes painful to express, and I wasn't sure I could adequately represent or convey the needs of so many others. But the moment I met the people in our group, I immediately felt at ease, comfortable. They understood. They cared.

I have learned that this wonderful organization reaches out to caregivers and individuals with dementia in so many important ways. They offer outreach programs for members who are struggling to care for loved ones. They distribute MedicAlert® + Safe Return® bracelets for those with dementia who may wander from their homes. They provide free, confidential family consultations and educational programs. Their Web site www.alz.org will help you locate Alzheimer's Association chapters throughout the United States.

Every year in Washington, D.C., the Alzheimer's Association holds their Annual Public Policy Forum—a gathering of advocates from all over the U.S. coming together in a common cause, asking members of Congress to support legislation that would lead to effective new drugs and an eventual cure for this horrible disease.

I was privileged to be chosen as a speaker at the Candlelight Vigil held at this event. Traditionally held at the Lincoln Memorial by the Reflecting Pool, this ceremony is a beautiful tribute to our loved ones and to those who have chosen to care for them. In accepting this incredible honor, I was able to share with so many others my feelings and hope that those like my father and Patrick will not be forgotten, but rather that their painful struggle will serve to give us strength as we continue in our efforts to wipe out Alzheimer's.

If you are caring for a loved one with Alzheimer's, you may sometimes feel overwhelmed. It may all seem too big, too much. If you need help, consider calling the Alzheimer's Association's Contact Center 24/7 Helpline. This toll-free service has trained professionals who can answer even basic questions, make suggestions about dealing with the challenges of caregiving, provide emotional support, and guide you toward care options. Call anytime at 1-800-272-3900.

You are not alone.

Marilynn Garzione

Visit Marilynn on her website and blog:
www.releasedtotheangels.com

Notes